How to Open & Operate a Financially Successful

Personal Financial Planning Business

WITH COMPANION CD-ROM

By Peg Stomierowski and Kristie Lorette
Edited by Martha Maeda

How to Open & Operate a Financially Successful Personal Financial Planning Business: With Companion CD-ROM

Copyright © 2012 by Atlantic Publishing Group, Inc.
1405 SW 6th Ave. • Ocala, Florida 34471 • 800-814-1132 • 352-622-1875–Fax
Website: www.atlantic-pub.com • E-mail: sales@atlantic-pub.com
SAN Number: 268-1250

Library of Congress Cataloging-in-Publication Data

Stomierowski, Peg, 1949-
  How to open & operate a financially successful personal financial planning business : with companion CD-ROM / by Peg Stomierowski and Kristie Lorette.
     p. cm.
  Includes bibliographical references and index.
  ISBN-13: 978-1-60138-334-1 (alk. paper)
  ISBN-10: 1-60138-334-7 (alk. paper)
  1. Financial planners. 2. Investment advisors. 3. Financial planners--United States. 4. Investment advisors--United States. I. Lorette, Kristie, 1975- II. Title. III. Title: How to open and operate a financially successful personal financial planning business.
  HG179.5.S757 2010
  332.6068--dc22

                              2010037202

Printed in the United States

PROJECT MANAGER: Gretchen Pressley • gpressley@atlantic-pub.com
BOOK PRODUCTION DESIGN: T.L. Price • design@tlpricefreelance.com
PROOFREADER: C&P Marse • bluemoon6749@bellsouth.net
FRONT COVER DESIGN: Meg Buchner • megadesn@mchsi.com
BACK COVER DESIGN: Jackie Miller • millerjackiej@gmail.com

Printed on Recycled Paper

A few years back we lost our beloved pet dog Bear, who was not only our best and dearest friend but also the "Vice President of Sunshine" here at Atlantic Publishing. He did not receive a salary but worked tirelessly 24 hours a day to please his parents.

Bear was a rescue dog who turned around and showered myself, my wife, Sherri, his grandparents Jean, Bob, and Nancy, and every person and animal he met (well, maybe not rabbits) with friendship and love. He made a lot of people smile every day.

We wanted you to know a portion of the profits of this book will be donated in Bear's memory to local animal shelters, parks, conservation organizations, and other individuals and nonprofit organizations in need of assistance.

– Douglas & Sherri Brown

PS: We have since adopted two more rescue dogs: first Scout, and the following year, Ginger. They were both mixed golden retrievers who needed a home.

Want to help animals and the world? Here are a dozen easy suggestions you and your family can implement today:

- *Adopt and rescue a pet from a local shelter.*
- *Support local and no-kill animal shelters.*
- *Plant a tree to honor someone you love.*
- *Be a developer — put up some birdhouses.*
- *Buy live, potted Christmas trees and replant them.*
- *Make sure you spend time with your animals each day.*
- *Save natural resources by recycling and buying recycled products.*
- *Drink tap water, or filter your own water at home.*
- *Whenever possible, limit your use of or do not use pesticides.*
- *If you eat seafood, make sustainable choices.*
- *Support your local farmers market.*
- *Get outside. Visit a park, volunteer, walk your dog, or ride your bike.*

Five years ago, Atlantic Publishing signed the Green Press Initiative. These guidelines promote environmentally friendly practices, such as using recycled stock and vegetable-based inks, avoiding waste, choosing energy-efficient resources, and promoting a no-pulping policy. We now use 100-percent recycled stock on all our books. The results: in one year, switching to post-consumer recycled stock saved 24 mature trees, 5,000 gallons of water, the equivalent of the total energy used for one home in a year, and the equivalent of the greenhouse gases from one car driven for a year.

Table of Contents

Chapter 2: Evaluating Your Strengths and Finding Your Niche 43

Chapter 3: Setting Up Your Business 57

Chapter 4: Writing a Business Plan...93

Chapter 5: Financing and Insuring Your Business.....................121

Chapter 6: Finding a Location and Setting Up Your Office 151

Chapter 7: Pricing, Payment, and Managing Costs 179

Chapter 8: Marketing Your Financial Planning Business............199

Chapter 9: Winning and Retaining Clients 227

Chapter 10: Hiring Employees and Office Support Services 247

Conclusion 261

Appendix A: What is Your
Preference? 263

Appendix B: Sample Articles of
Organization...................................269

Appendix C: Insurance Checklist 275

Appendix D: Sample Client
Intake Forms 277

Appendix E: Sample Financial
Planning Agreement.........................279

Foreword

The decision to become an independent financial planner is a big one. Our profession requires so many talents. The topics that we deal with, by their very nature, are complex and constantly evolving. The client, or customer, who is the recipient of our services often looks to us because they do not have the time, or ability, to understand the issues at hand. A financial planner must master the art of being part number cruncher, part trusted adviser, and sometimes part confidant. Average planners can do one; a great planner can do all three.

Do not go into this business solely to make money. If you do, you will fail. As you will see in the numerous case studies in these pages, the best planners have a passion for helping people. The best independent planners get as much satisfaction from helping a client reach their goals as they do from earning a good living and being their own boss. Clients feel this passion and find comfort in knowing they have "someone in their corner." These clients become their adviser's best source of new business as they tell friends and associates about him or her. Word of mouth is more important to an independent financial planner than almost any other business owner.

As an independent financial planner, the product is YOU. Your advice. With greater use of the Internet, more people are better educated about the generalities of personal finance. Because the basic level of knowledge a potential client brings to the initial meeting is so much higher than it used to be, someone can form an opinion in seconds about the quality of your advice and whether you are going to be able to help. Fifteen years ago, it was "who you know" that differentiated planners. Now, "what you know" is as much a part of the equation.

After gaining more knowledge of financial planning and the experience to deliver your services to clients, opening your own independent financial planning business may be the next logical step. This book will help you navigate through the various issues involved with opening an independent financial planning practice. Think of it as "the business of running my business."

**Cass Chappell, co-founder Chappell,
Mayfield & Associates, Atlanta, Georgia**

As co-founder of Chappell, Mayfield & Associates, Cass Chappell counsels individual investors, families and small businesses on financial planning, wealth accumulation, retirement and estate planning, education savings, insurance planning, business continuation planning, employee benefits, and more.

Cass launched his financial planning career as an agent for Prudential Financial in 1996 and quickly moved to a manager position in the company's financial services division. Cass

holds the CFP®, CLU®, and ChFC® designations, which reflects his commitment to excellence in investment decision-making and financial planning. He also holds a B.S. in management from Georgia Tech.

With works published in numerous personal finance and financial planning publications, Cass is dedicated to educating, and thereby empowering, investors of all ages and in all stages of their financial planning process.

Cass lives in Atlanta, Georgia with his wife Alison and daughter Olivia.

To find out more, please visit **www.ChappellMayfield.com** or his blog **www.atlantaplanningguys.com**.

Introduction

Personal financial planning is unlike any other career in the financial industry because it involves you directly in the lives of your individual clients. In addition to designing portfolios and tax shelters, a financial planner helps clients with personal goals, such as providing for a special-needs dependent, funding retirement, or saving for a child's college education. At times, a financial planner even becomes a life coach and encourages clients to make lifestyle changes that will improve their financial situations. Interacting with clients on such a personal level can be deeply satisfying. A financial planner also interacts a great deal with the local community by networking with clients and local business people and becoming involved in professional associations.

If you have a college degree and a background in accounting, economics, securities, retirement planning, tax advising, mutual funds, or sales of financial products such as annuities and life insurance, you have the basic skills to become a personal financial planner. However, opening and operating your own business will require you to take on multiple roles.

Independence comes at a price — you can no longer go home at 5 p.m. every afternoon and forget about your job. Your drive and initiative will expand the business by attracting and winning over new clients. When you stop networking, the business stops. On top of the work you do for your clients, you will be responsible for keeping accounts, filing and paying taxes, maintaining licenses and registrations, complying with federal, state and local regulations, and hiring and managing employees.

This book is an overview of all the things that must be done to open a new financial planning business. Because each topic only can be covered briefly, you will find references throughout the book to websites where you can find additional information. These websites are listed in a directory, *Further Reading*, at the end of the book. The *Appendixes* and the *Companion CD* contain templates, sample documents and contracts, forms, and checklists you can modify and print for your own use.

CHAPTER 1

The Changing Role of Financial Planners

The primary role of a personal financial adviser is to help individuals meet their personal financial needs. Most people do not have the skills and knowledge necessary to manage every aspect of their financial affairs successfully. They may understand how to invest for retirement but know little about minimizing income tax on those investments, withdrawing income after they retire, or ensuring their property will go to their heirs in the future. A financial adviser is a trained professional who provides an overview of the client's financial situation, suggests ways to improve the client's future outcome, and helps the client implement strategies to accumulate and manage wealth.

A financial planner offers guidance about:

- Investments
- Tax laws
- Insurance decisions
- Short-term and long-term goal setting

- Retirement planning

- Education expense planning (usually for children of the clients)

Some financial advisers specialize in one particular area, such as estate planning, while others are generalists who help clients with their overall financial management.

Personal financial advisers not only need expertise in their financial fields but also the ability to attract and keep loyal clients. When first starting to build a customer base, a personal financial adviser may spend 50 percent of his or her time marketing financial services and scouting for prospective clients.

A financial adviser typically begins by gathering information from the client and then organizes it into a comprehensive written financial plan. The written financial plan includes recommendations that will allow the client to meet financial goals and points out problem areas along with solutions to rectify the problems. A personal financial adviser may also seek the advice of other professionals such as attorneys and accountants to ensure the plan is solid. The financial adviser then works with the client to implement the plan.

Most financial advisers possess licenses to sell clients financial products and services such as investments (stocks, bonds, and mutual funds) and insurance that help their clients achieve their goals.

The New Landscape
of Financial Planning

The profession of personal financial advising has existed for about 40 years, during which it has gone through several transformations. When the Investment Advisors Act of 1940, part of an effort to clean up the corrupt investment companies (now known as mutual funds), required investment advisers to register with the Securities and Exchange Commission (SEC), only 895 individuals applied for registration, and only 700 of them were accepted. At that time, investing in the stock market was regarded as a form of speculation and was done mainly by the financial elite. For ordinary people, the predominant investments were life insurance, real estate, and for some, mutual funds.

A need for individualized financial advice arose during the 1950s when servicemen returning from World War II and the Korean War created a market for financial products, and a thriving economy provided ordinary Americans with cash to invest.

In 1962, Congress passed the Self-Employed Individuals Retirement Act, which allowed the creation of individual tax-deferred retirement accounts known as Keogh Accounts for self-employed individuals. The Employee Retirement Income Security Act (ERISA) enacted in 1974 allowed anyone with earned income to set up a tax-deferred investment account. Until the 1970s, most employers funded retirement pensions for their employees, and in 1980, only 3,500 financial advisers were registered with the SEC.

In December 1969, Loren Dunton, a financial consultant from Colorado, and James R. Johnston, a life insurance salesman, established the International Association for Financial Planning (IAFP) and the College for Financial Planning to raise the standard of professionalism in the financial services industry. They recognized that the industry's emphasis on sales of life insurance and mutual funds must be replaced with an emphasis on giving financial advice and offering a selection of financial solutions. The first class of 42 Certified Financial Planners (CFPs) graduated from the College for Financial Planning in 1973. The work of the IAFP and the Institute of Certified Financial Planners (ICFP), which merged in 2000 to create the Financial Planning Association (FPA) (**www.fpanet.org**), helped establish personal financial planning as a recognized profession.

During the 1970s, rapid inflation and high taxes pushed financial advisers to focus primarily on setting up tax shelters for their clients and protecting their wealth from inflation. A common strategy was to set up a limited partnership in which the client invested in a business without actively participating in it and deducted business losses from the client's other taxable income. The bottom fell out of this strategy with the passage of the Taxpayer Relief Act of 1986. Passive business partners were no longer allowed to deduct business expenses from their other income, and these deductions were even made illegal retroactively. This was a blow to financial planners who had concentrated on tax shelters, and membership in the IAFP dropped from 25,000 to 10,000.

The widespread adoption of 401(k) plans during the 1980s shifted the burden of saving for retirement from employers to private individuals with tax-deferred investment accounts. The stock market boom, which began in 1982, stimulated interest in investment as a vehicle for creating wealth. Suddenly, there was a much greater demand for financial advisers who could help people make decisions about their investment portfolios and arrange their complex financial affairs.

During the late 1990s, the development of new technologies and the emergence of the Internet brought about major changes in the way people manage money. Information about individual stocks and mutual funds was no longer the closely guarded domain of stockbrokers and financial firms; anyone could do his or her own research and access detailed information on the Internet. Discount online brokerages allowed individuals to trade on the stock market for a fraction of the fees charged by traditional stock brokerages. Financial management software and online banking made it possible for individuals to easily assess and monitor their own finances. Many investment companies began offering their products directly to consumers online. Clients today tend to be much better informed about financial options than they were a decade ago. As commissions on sales of financial products shrank, finance professionals gravitated towards fee-based services and the cultivation of long-term, trusting relationships with clients.

The recession that began in 2007 created the need for new types of financial services as people's life savings evaporated, homes went into foreclosure, and many people found themselves faced with the need to make difficult choices and restructure their financial affairs. Today less than 25 percent of U.S. companies have pension plans, and as the first investors in 401(k) plans approach retirement age, many are finding their savings inadequate for their needs.

Recently, after a young financial planner addressed a group concerning his services, he was approached by a retiree, who said, "I have two attorneys and two CPAs that I spend a lot of money on ... what more can *you* do that they do not?"

The financial planner could not answer the question until he had the opportunity to meet with the retiree and go through the prospective client's intake sheet, which detailed all of the client's finances.

The financial planner reviewed the documents the client provided to him and immediately noted a few key problems, including improper beneficiary designations. The retiree's insurance was poorly structured, his tax decisions were not serving his needs, and many of his dreams were not likely to be realized if he continued down the same path. The financial planner worked with the client and quickly instituted changes, which resulted in the retiree's heirs standing to receive about $920,000 of the $3 million estate. Although the man's life insurance coverage was doubled, his annual premiums dropped by about two-thirds, and his tax bill was reduced by $40,000.

People in all walks of life can use these kinds of services to manage their finances. After an initial consultation, a client can usually expect to pay a fee to have the financial adviser prepare a customized financial plan, which reviews the client's overall financial resources and may include general insurance or investment recommendations. The client may choose not to use the services of the financial planner to fulfill all of the needs laid out in the financial plan. The client may implement one part of the plan now, allow the relationship to grow, and then, at some point in the future, begin to add in the other elements of the financial plan.

Earnings and Outlook: What to Expect

Now is a good time to open a financial planning business. The first wave of approximately 80 million baby boomers (people born during the explosion of births that occurred after World War II) began reaching retirement age around 2008 and will continue to retire in large numbers for the next two decades, which will increase the demand for retirement planning and financial advice.

The Bureau of Labor Statistics predicts that the availability of personal financial adviser positions with financial firms will increase by up to 30 percent during the next seven years. Although there is no official estimate for self-employed financial advisers, their numbers are also expected to increase substantially. Approximately 4 out of 10 personal financial advisers are self-employed.

A financial adviser's income comes from charging clients a flat-rate percentage of the assets under the planner's management. Other sources of income are hourly fees for services or fees charged for buying stocks or insurance products. In addition to their fees, financial advisers may receive commissions for products sold.

According to the U.S. Bureau of Labor Statistics, 149,460 personal financial advisers worked for financial firms in the U.S. in 2009. Their annual mean wages ranged from $146,460 in New York to $64,810 in Florida, with many companies paying additional bonuses based on their annual profits. These statistics did not include self-employed financial advisers.

Many firms advertising to hire financial advisers list an average base pay between $35,375 and $74,861 a year and stress that the rest of the income is earned from sales functions. These firms typically train candidates and help get them licensed.

When you start building your own practice, do not expect an income from the business right away. It could take from 18 months to three years to begin making money and at least five years to build a profitable operation. If you already have an established track record in financial services, you may be able to acquire clients and accumulate substantial assets under your management quickly, but you still need the acumen to run a business wisely.

CASE STUDY: BIG FIRMS ARE GOOD PLACES TO CUT YOUR TEETH BEFORE HANGING SINGLE

Cass Chappell, CFP®, co-founder and president
Chappell, Mayfield & Associates, LLC
3200 Cobb Galleria Parkway, Suite 215
Atlanta, GA 30339
www.chappellmayfield.com
Cass@chappellmayfield.com
Phone: 770-980-1717
Fax: 770-980-1867

Cass Chappell wanted his work to actually mean something to the people he worked with. He wanted the work to be fulfilling, not just the bottom line of another company. Chappell was impressed by how rewarded he felt when he helped people and they appreciated what he had done for them. He was also seeking a career that paid him for performance and one that permitted his entrepreneurial spirit to shine. For Chappell, the perfect solution was to branch off and create his own financial planning business. "At the end of the day, our work matters to another person," Chappell said. "It is not business to business, in which a faceless corporation is the benefactor of my work."

According to Chappell, many assumptions are made about financial planners: They only work with people who have substantial sums of money to invest, or they are essentially glorified stockbrokers. His clients know that this could not be further from the truth.

Chappell is able to prove to his clients, time and again, that he really cares about them and their affairs, to the point where they worry for *his* sake when they suffer losses. On four separate occasions over the course of the recent economic recession, Chappell had clients — some of whom were losing six-figure sums — call to express concern that he might be distressed over their situations.

"During the height of the financial crisis, we were sending e-mails almost daily," Chappell said. "These e-mails were meant to educate our clients on the current state of the markets and to help promote prudent investment behavior. In other words, we wanted to help our clients avoid the urge to take money out of the market at precisely the wrong time. Many of our clients did not look at their account values on a daily basis, but they did see our e-mails. Some could tell, from the tone, that the crisis was taking a toll on us as advisers. In other words, they seemed to think *we* were stressing out as stewards for their money. On these four occasions, the clients called us to give *us* a pep talk. This would not be the case if we did not have a solid relationship with these clients."

To alleviate any fears his clients might have for themselves, he works diligently with his clients during client performance reviews each quarter by giving out fundamental tips and re-emphasizing the long-term view. "Volatility or losses over a short period of time are not as important as focusing on the long-term goals," Chappell said.

Some of the most heart-warming cases Chappell has handled while at Chappell, Mayfield & Associates have involved widows who grew up during a time when women did not work and did not make investment decisions. He gets a thrill out of teaching them independence while helping to calm their anxiety over "being in charge."

Chappell graduated from Georgia Tech in 1996 with a Bachelor of Science degree in management (business). His first job was as an insurance agent with Prudential, where he sold all types of insurance and mutual funds. He earned the CLU (Chartered Life Underwriter) designation in 1997, the ChFC (Chartered Financial Consultant) in 1998, and the CFP (Certified Financial Planner) in 2003.

One night, Chappell went home after having drinks with friends and sat down in front of the TV. He was inspired by a commercial about financial planners going independent and made the move a month later. He partnered with a friend from college who had come into the insurance business at the same time as he had. This was in 2005, and Chappell says the move just felt right. He was 31 at the time and had started in the business at 23. He had seven or eight years of training and support before going independent. Still, Chappell and his partner were not in any position to go in and lose money. Fortunately, within six months, they were able to accumulate $20 million in assets under their dual management.

Chappell says there is no way he could have gotten into the financial planning industry without the years he spent in the insurance business. He could not imagine becoming a financial planner without having a background with a major institution such as a bank, an investment house, or an insurance company. He advises that you get your feet wet at a similar institution before striking out on your own. They will pay your salary while you learn, which will help to lessen the pressure.

One of the things he likes to clarify right away is that "financial planner" is a very broad term. For the most part, financial planners, particularly those who have earned the CFP, or Certified Financial Planner certification, are not stock pickers or Wall Street types.

People who work at certain well-known investment firms and are primarily investment advisers may call themselves "financial planners," but that is not the way Chappell uses the term. At the end of the day, a financial planning business model is based on accumulating assets. The best way to do financial planning is to be unbiased and objective. If you are working for a large corporation, you cannot really be independent.

However, Chappell does admit that being independent can be lonely. Chappell's firm consists only of himself, his partner, and a couple of other employees. They only see other planners at industry gatherings about best practices, which is why he says you need a solid understanding of the industry before setting up shop.

To Chappell, the three most important factors in opening and operating a successful financial planning business are:

1. Knowledge. You must know your stuff. This is not just another sales job.

2. Passion for being a "student of the game."

3. Straightforward and honest dealings with your clients. This is extremely important.

The sound fundamentals he would recommend for any younger client are the very same principles he has lived his own life by: Buy a lot of term life insurance and save as much as you can afford. Although many of Chappell's clients pay him a fee to produce a written financial plan, this service may not be necessary for everyone. Younger clients, those whose financial situations have not fully taken shape yet, are usually better served by protecting their assets (through insurance) and saving as much as possible.

For the most part, Chappell has never been troubled by legal concerns. Although he does have business insurance to cover any legal issues, he is thorough in documenting conversations and correspondence with clients. He feels if he does right by people, there will not be any issues.

Credentials and Working Conditions

Continued education is important in the field of financial planning because many aspects of the discipline are constantly changing. A degree is preferred — a bachelor's (often in accounting, finance, economics, business, math, or law) or a master's in fields related to finance or business administration — but is not always a requirement to work in the field. There are many avenues for obtaining additional professional credentials.

Many planners earn other professional designations, including CFP (Certified Financial Planner). Issued by the Certified Financial Planner Board of Standards (**www.cfp.net**), this requires several years of relevant experience and completion of certain education requirements, including a bachelor's degree, a comprehensive examination, and adherence to a code of ethics. The exam tests the candidate's knowledge of the financial planning process, insurance, risk management, employee benefits planning, taxes, retirement planning, investment, and estate planning. Candidates are also required to have a working knowledge of debt management, planning liability, emergency fund reserves, and statistical modeling.

Some CFPs who also work with companies as financial analysts earn the CFA (Chartered Financial Analyst) designation, sponsored by the CFA Institute (**www.cfainstitute.org**). Wealth managers who work with wealthy individuals or institutes frequently earn this certification. The requirements are a bachelor's degree or four years of relevant work experience and three examinations covering topics such as accounting, economics, securities, financial markets and instruments, corporate finance, asset valuation, and portfolio management.

The Financial Industry Regulatory Authority (FINRA) is the licensing organization for the securities industry, found at **www.finra.org**. According to government data, many personal financial planners hold Series 7, 63, and 66 licenses and are affiliated with large securities firms; many also hold insurance licenses issued by state licensing boards. Many people in the financial services industry obtain a license to sell securities or recommend investments. Testing commonly involves the Series 7 license, which allows someone to act as a registered representative of a firm; Series 63 and 66 licenses allow holders to legally give financial advice. Series 7 is a corequisite in addition to the Series 66 exam before you can register with the state.

Accredited Investment Fiduciary® (AIF®), offered through Fi360, an organization providing investment fiduciary education (**www.fi360.com**) designates someone who demonstrates knowledge and competency in the area of fiduciary responsibility. To qualify as an AIF, you must complete a specialized program on fiduciary standards as well as pass stringent testing. Many other professional designations also are available.

Common Certifications for Financial Planners

Certification	Administering Organization	Description
Accredited Investment Fiduciary (AIF) www.fi360.com/main/designations_aif.jsp	fi360	Demonstrates knowledge and competency in the area of fiduciary responsibility and communicates a commitment to standards of investment fiduciary excellence. Holders of the AIF mark have successfully completed a specialized program on investment fiduciary standards and subsequently passed a comprehensive examination.
Certified Financial Planner (CFP) www.cfp.net/become/certification.asp	Certified Financial Planner Board of Standards	Mastery of nearly 100 integrated financial planning topics, exam, work experience, adherence to CFP Board's Standards of Professional Conduct, ongoing education, and disclosure requirements

Certification	Administering Organization	Description
Certified Financial Planner Board of Standards, the Personal Financial Specialist (CPA/PFS)	American Institute of Certified Public Accountants (AICPA)	Must obtain the CPA License, be a member in good standing of the AICPA, enroll in comprehensive PFP education, attain a specified level of PFP experience, pass a PFP Examination
www.aicpa.org/InterestAreas/ PersonalFinancialPlanning/Membership/ Pages/OverviewofthePersonalFinancialSpecial ist(PFS)Credential.aspx		
CIMA Certificate in Business Accounting	Investment Management Consultants Association (IMCA)	Qualifies candidate for membership in CIMA, focused on business accounting
www.cimaglobal.com/Students/ Entry-level-certificate-in-business-accounting/		
Form ADV	U.S. Securities and Exchange Commission	The form used by investment advisers to register with both the Securities and Exchange Commission (SEC) and state securities authorities
www.sec.gov/about/forms/formadv-part1a.pdf		
Registration	National Association of Personal Financial Advisors (NAPFA)	To register as a member, you must have three years of comprehensive financial planning experience, ADV and approval of a financial plan created for a client
www.napfa.org/JoinNAPFA.asp		

Certification	Administering Organization	Description
Series 63, Uniform Securities Agent State Law Examination www.nasaa.org/industry___regulatory_resources/exams/474.cfm	North American Securities Administrators Association (NASAA)	Developed by North American Securities Administrators Association (NASAA) and FINRA, qualifies candidates to act as securities agents within a state
Series 66, NASAA-Uniform Combined State Law Exam (AG and/or RA) www.nasaa.org/industry___regulatory_resources/exams/733.cfm	North American Securities Administrators Association (NASAA)	Qualifies candidates as both securities agents and investment adviser representatives
Series 7, General Securities Representative Exam www.finra.org/web/groups/industry/@ip/@comp/@regis/documents/industry/p038201.pdf	Financial Industry Regulatory Authority (FINRA)	Allows someone to act as a registered representative of a firm; covers a broad range of investments including stocks, bonds, options, limited partnerships, and investment company products

No two days are the same

Although personal financial advisers usually work standard business hours, a financial adviser typically does not have a set daily routine. The work varies from day to day and week to week. It may include early or late meetings with clients, at their convenience, and scheduled seminars and planning sessions. Independents value the flexibility of owning their own businesses.

A day in the life of a financial planner

Ted Schwartz, an investment adviser at Capstone Investment Financial Group in Colorado Springs, works more on the investment side than many of his fellow CFPs. The following is a description of a typical day for him:

- 8 a.m.–9 a.m.: Review e-mail and place trades to rebalance client accounts.

- 9 a.m.–10 a.m.: Discussion with a new client who has inherited money. He is concerned about the recent market downturn.

- 10 a.m.–11 a.m.: Prepare for client teleconference.

- 11a.m.–12 p.m.: Use Web conferencing software to go over financial plan with a client who has moved out of the state.

- 12 p.m.: Lunch

- 1 p.m.–2 p.m.: Review market, trades, and e-mail.

- 2 p.m.–3 p.m.: Work on writing blog for his website.

- 3 p.m.–4 p.m.: Update data in performance reporting software. New client setup, etc.

- 4 p.m.–5 p.m.: Meeting with client. Review new account paperwork, and discussion of Roth conversion for 2010.

Alexandra Armstrong, a financial planner at a four-partner Washington, D.C., firm, reserves most morning hours to answer e-mail, telephone messages, and other correspondence. She might combine lunch with a lecture by a speaker from an investment firm on a specific investment or a trend in the industry. Most afternoons, she schedules client meetings at 2 p.m. and 4 p.m., with current client meetings averaging about one hour and new client meetings about two hours. Each month, with the support of specialists in her office, she is able to send 20 to 30 reports out to clients with written recommendations for them to make changes or implement financial plans. A letter advising clients on the cost of each service accompanies the recommendations. Once clients agree to proceed with the recommended service, Alexandra devotes of a portion of her time to implementing the strategy for the client.

CASE STUDY: LEARNING TO BALANCE CLIENTS, FAMILY, AND COMMUNITY

Kasey Gahler, CFP, owner
Gahler Financial
4807 Spicewood Springs Rd., Bldg. 2, Suite 113
Austin, TX 78758
www.gahlerfinancial.com
kasey@gahler-financial.com
Phone: 512-302-9995
Fax: 512-795-0667

In 1996, after one semester in college as an accounting major, Gahler realized he could not be a bean counter for the rest of his life. He quickly discovered he enjoyed face-to-face interactions and building close relationships with clients. In Gahler's freshman year, he changed his major to financial planning. At that time, the university Gahler attended was one of fewer than a dozen colleges that offered this specific major.

Gahler graduated and started with an insurance-based planning firm in 2002. After six years there, Gahler entered private practice. He wanted to emphasize an advisory, financial planning approach over sales. Gahler has been practicing for eight years now, passed the CFP board exam in early 2009, and specializes in working with physician specialists.

As in any niche, you must know your prospects and customers, and Gahler spent time learning about medicine, what doctors deal with day to day, and their financial concerns. The specific financial needs of physicians differ significantly from those of the public. Many have a shorter time span for retirement and college planning, face higher risk of lawsuits, and are coping with a quickly changing medical environment. To fulfill his client needs, Gahler has become well versed in asset protection. He devotes time to understanding how changes in medicine, coupled with the potential for declining incomes, might impact his clients in the short and long term.

Gahler has no doubt that financial planning is his true calling in life. He enjoys visiting with clients, discussing their goals, and making recommendations on how to accomplish them. Gahler finds it rewarding to see all of this unfold. Another reward of private practice is the flexibility to spend time with his family. Because his clients are spread out across the country, he regularly travels for work, and often his wife is able to join him. A typical workweek is about 40 to 55 hours, and it usually includes at least one day of travel. Monday is often reserved for preparation, and Friday tends to be the day he gets caught up on miscellaneous work. Gahler splits most weeks, working half of the time from the office and half from home. This scheduling flexibility, besides benefiting his family, allows Gahler to serve at church and charity events around town.

Gahler's biggest challenge is probably managing client expectations. Clients tend to focus on the here and now. It is harder in our fast-paced world to focus on the horizon and remember the past instead of getting wrapped up in what is going on in today's market and economy.

Like a surgeon who brings in a younger physician to share overhead costs and caseload, Gahler shares an administrative assistant, as well as office space, with another adviser who has been practicing for nearly 25 years. The two advisers have a synergistic working relationship, and Gahler learns a lot from the other adviser.

According to Gahler, financial planning involves providing a comprehensive picture of personal finances for the clients you serve. As a financial planner, you help clients set goals for the future and then help them strive to reach those goals. The rewards are not only the income you can earn as a financial adviser but also the satisfaction that comes from helping someone meet his or her financial goals.

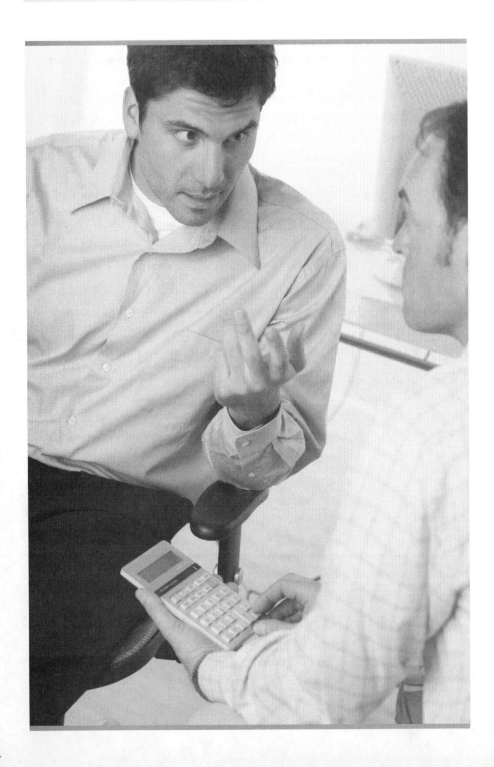

CHAPTER 2

Evaluating Your Strengths and Finding Your Niche

As a personal financial planner, the product you are selling is you. Your clients are entrusting you with their financial futures. They are relying on your expertise and skills to make the most of their resources and solve their problems. They are consulting you because you have the knowledge and experience they lack. If you do not have a solid background in finance, insurance, investment, tax laws, and estate planning, you have little to offer. Do not consider starting your own financial planning business until you have acquired the necessary education and experience.

A professional appearance and environment help attract clients and win their trust. A personal financial planner should have good relational and networking skills. He or she should project poise and confidence. Clients need to feel that the information they share with you is confidential and that they are safe in your hands. They should feel that you are easily accessible, and they can approach you at any time with questions and concerns. Because financial planning services usually include preparing financial assessments, you should be able to explain, without embellishment or evasion, how the various elements of a personal financial plan interact over time for the client's greatest benefit.

It is important to develop a reliable network of other professionals who can develop quotes and quickly answer questions. For example, a financial planner who does not sell insurance should have a strong working relationship with someone who does. A trustworthy personal financial planner knows when it is necessary to consult another professional for more information in order to protect a client's interests.

Education

Personal financial planners come from a variety of educational backgrounds. Most have a four-year college degree in a finance-related field, plus several years of work experience related to financial planning. Many advisers have a master's degree, typically in business administration or finance. Financial advisers who buy or sell insurance policies, stocks, or bonds, must obtain the applicable licenses from the states in which they practice. In addition, they may hold credentials including the Certified Financial Planner (CFP) issued by the Certified Financial Planner Board of Standards, the Personal Financial Specialist (CPA/PFS) credential from the American Institute of Certified Public Accountants (AICPA), or registration with the National Association of Personal Financial Advisers (NAPFA). To earn and keep these credentials, a financial planner not only must pass an examination but also adhere to a code of ethics and participate in continuing education programs.

Personal financial planners must be solidly versed in the fundamentals of managing their own and other people's money, including investments, cash, credit, savings, home equity, some basic real estate, and estate procedures and protections. They must know the basics of preparing taxes, understand how to balance assets and liabilities appropriately to manage risk, appreciate the issues involved in paying for a college education, and understand how to read financial documents. Financial planners also should be familiar with different forms of insurance, including life, health, disability, property/casualty, automobile, and renters insurance.

According to CollegeBoard.com (**www.collegeboard.com**), 60 colleges and universities now offer majors in financial planning, and an additional 15 offer majors in family resource management studies. Fields of study that can lead to a career in financial planning include basic economics, accounting, investment, statistics, and finance.

Typical Courses for a Financial Planning Major

Communication and Research Techniques for Master's Students

Financial Planning Process and Risk Management

Insurance

Investment Planning

Income Tax Planning

Retirement Planning

Estate Planning (Part I)

Estate Planning (Part II)

Portfolio Management for Personal Financial Planners

Tax Planning for the Highly Compensated

Preretirement Financial Planning Topics

Issues and Cases in Estate Planning

Personal Financial Planning: Integrated Case Study

Typical Courses for a Financial Planning Major

Financial Statement Analysis

Investment Analysis

Qualified Retirement Plan Topics

Estate Planning for Retirement Benefits

Women and Financial Planning

Money and Banking

Global Economics

Public Policy

Technical Analysis

Another important qualification for a financial planner, which cannot be measured by a written exam, is the ability to interact skillfully with clients. Financial planning education includes training in conducting interviews and making presentations, but only practice will develop your ability to gain a client's confidence, explain financial matters clearly and understandably in layman's terms, and manage the client's expectations. You must convince clients you know what you are doing but are willing to listen to what they say and address their concerns. Financial planning always involves an element of risk and uncertainty, and there will be times when the stock market slumps or investments do not perform as expected. At other times, a client may insist on doing something you believe is unwise. The way in which you handle those difficult moments ultimately will define the success of your business. Unhappy clients will leave you for another planner. An independent financial planner gets business through word-of-mouth; satisfied clients will refer their friends and colleagues, and your business will expand.

You may be considering a career in personal financial planning because you have experience working in related financial services jobs, because you have lost a job in another field, or because you desire a different kind of work experience. Some of the things that make personal financial planning an appealing career are:

- The potential for a high income
- The opportunity to do something you enjoy and are passionate about
- A satisfying work situation
- The ability to be your own boss
- A need for math skills
- Diverse groups of people
- The opportunity to provide financial advice to others
- The chance to help people
- The flexibility of setting your own schedule

Before you strike out on your own as an independent financial planner, however, you should gain experience by working for a company that sells investments, insurance or financial planning services. When you feel confident that you can make objective recommendations and offer your clients the best financial advice, you are ready to launch your own business. Maintain relationships with fellow financial planners in your area. Look for a mentor who knows the local market and can coach you for the first year or two.

FPA Mentorship

State and local chapters of the Financial Planning Association (FPA) offer mentorship programs. Experienced financial planners help to shape the careers of their future colleagues by interacting with financial planning students or planners who are transitioning to a private practice for one year. These mentors offer advice and the benefit of their experience, and they can help guide fellow financial planners through new experiences, such as setting up or buying a business or taking on a business partner. In addition, the FPA conducts weeklong residencies during which experienced mentors give new financial planners hands-on experience in dealing with clients. To learn about mentorship opportunities in your area, contact your local or state FPA chapter (**www.fpanet.org**).

Payment Models

Financial planners perform a broad range of services and follow a variety of business models. Some are specialists in a particular area, such as tax planning or investing for retirement. Others sell particular products such as annuities, investment portfolios, or insurance.

Financial planners follow several payment models:

Fee-only

The financial planner gets all of his or her income from fees and does not get commission from the sale of financial products. The planner may charge fixed rates for different services, an hourly fee, a percentage (typically 1

– 1.5 percent) of the assets placed under his or her management, or a fee based on how well a client's investments perform.

Commission-only

The financial planner does not charge any fees for consultations or the preparation of financial plans but gets commissions from the sale of financial products to the client.

Combination fee and commission

The financial planner charges fixed rates, an hourly fee, or percentage-based fees for consulting, preparing financial plans, and managing investments and may receive commissions from the sale of financial products.

Salary

A financial planner may receive a salary plus bonuses from a financial services firm.

Your business model and whether you sell financial products or just manage investments on behalf of your clients will determine your payment structure.

Knowing Your Competitive Advantage

Your competitive advantage derives from services, characteristics, or traits you possess that surpass those of others. Identify your business with those characteristics, and focus on the qualities that set you apart from other financial planners with businesses similar to yours. For example, you may already have an extensive list of contacts from two decades in the insurance business, or you may be a woman- or minority-owned business. You might have a special understanding of the needs of a particular segment of your community. You might be an active member in a local church where you can easily network with retirees. Any of these circumstances would give you access to opportunities that might not be available to your competitors. When you decide on a location for your office, choose your décor, and plan your advertising, make choices that will emphasize your competitive advantage.

Mind your Ps & Qs — and your Cs

Business students are taught to pay attention to the Five Ps: procedures, products, place, pricing, and promotion. The following factors are also crucial to business success:

Passion: A successful business is more than just a business to a passionate founder. It is more like a calling.

Planning: A carefully constructed strategic plan provides a firm foundation and allows for flexible direction.

Quality: Alternately referred to as excellence

Communication. Good customer relations build loyalty.

Change. Thoughtful change management allows a business to roll with changes in the industry, technology, and market.

SWOT analysis is a strategic planning tool that generally involves examining enterprises from at least four angles: internal strengths and weaknesses and external opportunities and threats. You can use SWOT analysis to evaluate your business personality along with your business ideas.

Write down the answers to the following questions:

- What are your strengths in general?

- What are your strengths regarding the field of personal financial planning in particular?

- What do you have to offer?

- What do other people notice that you do really well?

- What do you love to do?

- What opportunities do you see reflected in your passions?

- On the other hand, what obstacles or threats do you perceive?

- What are your plans, and possible timetable, to overcome these weaknesses?

Review your written answers. You should be able to identify several strengths you can emphasize in your business. If you recognize weaknesses that could seriously inhibit your success, make a step-by-step plan to either overcome them or compensate for them. For example, if you are lacking knowledge in a particular field, plan to take some educational courses. If you do not know how to install and set up a computer software program, hire a part-time employee to help you.

Appendix A contains a personality quiz that can help you evaluate your personal strengths and weaknesses.

Find Your Niche

A niche market is a particular group of people who have similar needs and circumstances, such as retirees, young parents, or people in the military. As you begin to build a client list and work with individual clients, you probably will gravitate towards a particular type of client. The experience you gain from helping one person can be applied to others in similar circumstances. You gradually may build up specialized knowledge about a particular profession or financial product that makes you particularly qualified to serve a specific group of clients. In the field of personal financial planning, the opportunity to serve niche markets is almost unlimited. The case studies in this chapter illustrate two interesting examples of niche markets.

You already may have developed a potential niche through your personal experiences. If you share similar experiences with your clients, you are able to empathize with them and communicate effectively. For example, if you have been through a divorce and have succeeded at processing the experience productively, you might be effective at sharing what you have learned with others. You might discover you have developed a passion for helping others to get back on their feet financially.

A niche market is a segment of the mainstream market that you might want to specifically target because of your products, interests, or expertise. Niches to consider include debt management, retirement planning, portfolio recovery, special-needs parenting, helping elderly or infirm parents navigate retirement, access to higher education, veteran issues, estate issues, tax advice, and financial planning for physicians. It is easier to target advertising to a niche market because you can select only those publications and websites read by your clients. There is a potential for charging higher prices in niche markets because people are willing to a pay premium for the advice and services of a professional who specializes in their specific situation.

CASE STUDY: NAVIGATING THE EMOTIONAL SIDE OF MONEY

Linda Leitz, CFP, EA, CDFA
(Certified Financial Planner, Enrolled
Agent, Certified Divorce Financial
Analyst)
Financial planner and co-owner
Pinnacle Financial Concepts
www.lindaleitz.com
linda@lindaleitz.com
719-260-9800

Linda Leitz is a personal financial planner whose Colorado-based firm has a stated niche working with divorced individuals and surviving spouses. Linda says working with upset and grieving people has taught her a lot.

During the divorce period, her firm works temporarily with one spouse or both on how to divide their assets. Although this represents a relatively small percentage of total revenue for the firm, she estimates that the long-term financial planning that occurs after the death of a spouse or after a divorce settlement represents one third to one half of the firm's revenues.

Divorce cases, in Linda's experience, tend to fall into several categories, including individuals with high net worth, professionals with stay-at-home spouses, codependents, and those ready to just divide the property and get it over with. Going through a divorce or the loss of a loved one is almost always a difficult situation for the client.

Because of this, general relationship skills are important for the financial planner, such as knowing the difference between extending sympathy and extending compassion. Although sympathizing could mean condoning a client's feelings of guilt, blame, and victimization, Leitz sees extending compassion as trying to help clients get out of negative perceptions and situations and get back onto their feet.

Clients in these situations often experience grief, so skills in grief counseling are useful for a financial planner who works with people going through breakups and deaths. Leitz says she went through mediation training soon after starting to do divorce financial consulting.

Although some very resilient people are quick to move on, she says others, especially those who did not instigate their divorces and often do not wish to be released from their marital vows, may spend years — even decades — attempting to recover from the scars of these broken dreams. Leitz says it appears as if some never fully heal.

People assume financial planning is all about numbers. However, if a financial planner does not understand the deeply emotional and personal aspects of money in someone's life, he or she is in the wrong profession. What drew Leitz to financial planning is the ability to help people make wise financial choices and develop a comfortable relationship with money. What keeps her in it is the combination of intellectual rewards and the close personal relationships she develops with clients. Most of Leitz's clients consider her an important part of their lives.

For Leitz, working with people who are divorcing means helping people grow into their own sense of autonomy and freedom. What she loves about being a financial planner is helping convince people they are going to be just fine (or if they do not feel fine, how to improve their circumstances). The peace of mind clients get from working with her is one of Leitz's biggest rewards. Working with people in and after divorce, or with someone whose spouse has died, offers some of the hardest work and greatest satisfaction in financial planning.

Setting Up Your Business

Before you can open your doors and welcome your first clients, you must lay the groundwork for your financial planning business. In addition to your professional certifications, you must obtain the required local, state, and federal licenses and registrations to carry out your business activities. The financial industry is highly regulated, and you are liable if you sell financial products without the proper registration and oversight. When you work for a bank or a firm that sells financial products, the company takes care of filing registrations and annual reports with federal and state agencies. As an independent, you are responsible for knowing the requirements and making sure you are legally qualified to offer financial services to your clients. If you plan to sell stocks and bonds, mutual funds, annuities, or insurance, you must comply with the federal and state regulations governing those industries.

In addition to obtaining licenses and registrations to sell financial products, you will have to obtain a local business license and arrange to pay state and local business taxes. You also will need to organize and register your business as a legal entity. The legal structure of your business will affect how you pay your income taxes and the extent to which you are personally liable for any legal action brought against you.

Many companies offer services to help you set up your business — for a substantial fee. You can save money by doing most things yourself. Often, all you have to do is fill out some online forms, pay a fee, and in some cases, provide documentation, such as a driver's license or proof of a business license. Federal, state, and local government websites walk you step-by-step through the registration process and provide telephone contacts or live chats to answer your questions. If you encounter difficulties you cannot resolve by yourself, you often can get assistance from your local U.S. Small Business Administration (SBA) office. The SBA website (**www.sba.gov**) offers valuable guidance. Standard templates are available for articles of incorporation and other registration documents. *See the companion CD for samples of these documents.*

Filling out your own registration forms helps you to understand the legal obligations of a business and may force you to think through aspects you might not have considered, such as how decisions will be made in a partnership and the responsibilities of each partner. You will also know how to alter your business organization in the future and know when reports and annual fees are due without depending on a third party who will charge you additional sums to do this work.

If you need to customize legal documents, you can pay a business lawyer by the hour to advise you. Do as much of the work as you can yourself and prepare your questions in advance so you will be able to explain your needs clearly to the lawyer and quickly determine what needs to be done.

CASE STUDY: PUTTING THE CLIENTS' INTERESTS IN LINE WITH YOUR OWN

Ted Schwartz, CFP
Capstone Investments
615 N. Nevada Ave.
Colorado Springs, CO 80903
www.capstoneinvest.com
ted@capstoneinvest.com

For Ted Schwartz, financial planning is a third career. He previously worked in mental health programs and then sold fine art for more than 15 years. Financial planning gave Schwartz the ability to combine his love of working with people with his acumen for numbers and data analysis. Schwartz holds a B.A. from Duke University, an M.A. from Oregon State, and completed the College for Financial Planning CFP program. Schwartz has had the privilege of assisting many individuals who have entrusted him with their hard-earned savings. Schwartz considers it an honor to be entrusted in this manner and strives every day to be worthy of the honor. He regards financial planning as a field in which you can experience the joys and challenges of continuous improvement. Because the field is constantly evolving, you can always learn more and be a bit better than you were the year before.

According to Schwartz, the first three rules in the financial planning business are:

1. Put the client's interests first.

2. Put the client's interests first.

3. Put the client's interests first.

Years ago, Schwartz read a book by a Canadian planner. His advice was simple but profound — he referred to the "Client 99" — that at all times, 99 percent of your focus needs to be on the client. This is the path to your success. If you focus on your success rather than the clients' success, neither party will come out well.

There is a great deal of potential liability attached to financial planning. Schwartz believes you can do what you truly believe is in the clients' best interests and still get into hot water.

Before the current recession set in, Schwartz says mainstream financial planning had too easily adopted the mantra of the financial services companies — to just "buy and hold" investments. Planners have to learn how to manage risk for their clients. If they fail to do that, Schwartz questions whether they should charge fees based on investment accounts as opposed to just charging for planning. Schwartz knows some great planners who are not capable investment managers, and vice versa. He believes professionals should only charge for the services in which they are experts.

Structuring Your Business

The legal structure of your business determines how you operate, what type of documents you must file, and how many and what type of documents are accessible for public scrutiny. If you are starting your business on your own, you will probably set it up as a sole proprietorship in the beginning. Most financial planning businesses begin as sole proprietorships, partnerships, or LLCs (limited liability companies). A corporation usually is not formed unless you decide to seek financing from outside investors, or your company becomes an employee-owned business.

Sole proprietorship

A sole proprietorship is owned and operated by one person who exercises absolute control of operations. Most U.S. businesses begin as sole proprietorships. Under a sole proprietorship, you own 100 percent of the business, its assets, and its liabilities. As the owner, you are responsible for securing monetary backing, and you are ultimately responsible for any legal actions against your business.

A sole proprietorship is relatively inexpensive to set up, and with the exception of a couple of extra tax forms, there is no requirement to file complicated tax returns in addition to your own. Your business expenses can be deducted from your income for tax purposes. Until your business is bringing in a profit, a sole proprietorship is the easiest structure to maintain. As a sole proprietor, you can operate under your own name or do business under another name (fictitious name). Legal fees for starting the business will be lower than those for the other forms of business because fewer documents are required, and the owner has absolute authority over all business decisions.

Partnership

A partnership is almost as easy to establish as a sole proprietorship, with a few exceptions. Profits and losses are shared among partners. The two most common types of partnerships are general and limited partnerships. A general partnership can be formed by an oral agreement between two or more persons, but a legal partnership agreement drawn up by an attorney is advisable.

Not all partners in a partnership necessarily have equal ownership of the business. Normally, the extent of each partner's financial contribution to the business determines the percentage of the business that partner owns. This percentage is applied to sharing the organization's revenues as well as its financial and legal liabilities.

A primary difference between a partnership and a sole proprietorship is that the business does not cease to exist with the death of a partner. A deceased partner's share can be taken over by a new partner, or the partnership can be reorganized to accommodate the change. In either case, the business is able to continue without much disruption. Many partnerships take out a life insurance policy for each partner that allows the partnership to buy his or her share from the heirs in case of a partner's death.

Legal fees for drawing up a partnership agreement are higher than those for a sole proprietorship, but they are usually lower than fees for incorporation. A formal partnership agreement helps to solve disputes that might arise later on. Each partner is responsible for the other partners' business actions, as well as his or her own.

Generally, it is in the best interest of all partners to have an attorney develop a partnership agreement. Partnership agreements are simple legal documents that include such information as a business's name and purpose, its legal address, how long the partnership is intended to last, and the partners' names. It addresses partners' professional and financial contributions and how profits and losses will be distributed. The document needs to disclose plans for handling such changes as the death or addition of a partner or the selling of one partner's interest to another individual. The agreement should address how assets and liabilities will be distributed in case the partnership is dissolved.

A Partnership Agreement should include the following:

- Type of business

- Amount of money or property invested by each partner

- Responsibilities or duties of each partner

- How profit or loss will be divided among partners

- How each partner will receive compensation (salaries or a percentage of profits)

- How assets will be distributed when partnership is dissolved

- How long the partnership will continue

- Procedures for changing or dissolving the partnership

- How disputes will be settled

- What restrictions will be placed on each partner's authority to make decisions and to spend money?

- How the partnership will be reorganized if one of the partners dies or becomes incapacitated

Financial planning partnerships tend to form in one of two ways. In some instances, financial planners work together at a firm and then decide to start their own business together as a partnership. In other circumstances, a financial planner may start as a sole proprietor and then turn the business into a partnership when and if he or she meets another financial planner who complements the first partner's professional work.

Worksheet for a successful partnership

Before entering into a partnership, it is important that all partners agree on important matters such as compensation, decision-making, and reinvestment in the business. The following exercise will help you and your future partner(s) understand each other's expectations:

Finish these sentences and have your partner do the same. Then trade worksheets and discuss your opinions and answers to the following topics:

1. My philosophical vision for the company is…

2. My business strategy is…

3. I came to this strategy through the following education, practice, and life lessons:

4. My work ethic is _____

5. What "commitment to the business" means to me:

6. My talents are…

7. My partner's talents are…

8. My skills are…

9. My partner's skills are…

10. My role as I see it in the company is…

11. My partner's role in the company is…

12. Our method of compensation for partners is…

13. Our compensation plan for key employees and other employees involves...

14. Our recordkeeping will be done through _____ (method) or by _____ (person).

15. We plan to create capital by...

16. We will finance debt through these methods...

17. When big decisions need to be made, we will...

18. If we disagree on a decision that has a major impact on the company, we will...

19. Things we enjoy outside of working hours include...

Limited liability company

A limited liability company (LLC), often wrongly referred to as limited liability corporation, is not a corporation, but it offers many of the same advantages. Many small business owners and entrepreneurs prefer LLCs because they combine the limited liability protection of a corporation with the "pass through" taxation of a sole proprietorship or partnership, which means each owner pays personal income tax on his or her share of the profits instead of the company as a whole paying tax. The owners of an LLC, referred to as members, enjoy the same protection from liability as a corporation and the flexible recordkeeping of a partnership, which is not required to keep meeting minutes or records. In an LLC, the members are not personally liable for the debts incurred for and by the company, and profits can be distributed as the members deem appropriate. All expenses, losses, and profits are passed through the business to the individual members who ultimately pay either business taxes or personal taxes, but not both on the same income.

Owners of an LLC are called members and can be individuals, corporations, other LLCs, or foreign entities. In some instances, an LLC only contains one member (one owner). *Publication 3402, Tax Issues for Limited Liability Companies*, available on the IRS Web site (**www.irs.gov**) provides specific information on the tax return forms LLCs must file and how to handle employment taxes.

LLCs are a comparatively modern type of legal structure; the first one was established in Wyoming in 1977. It was not until 1988, when the Internal Revenue Service ruled the LLC business structure would be treated as a partnership for tax purposes, that other states followed suit by enacting their own statutes establishing the LLC form of business. LLCs are now allowed in all 50 states and Washington, D.C. An LLC is easier to establish than a corporation but requires more legal paperwork than a sole proprietorship. It is appropriate for a business whose operations require adequate protection from legal and financial liabilities for its members, but it is not large enough to warrant the expenses incurred in becoming a corporation or the recordkeeping involved in operating as a corporation.

Regulations and procedures affecting forming LLCs differ from state to state, and they can be found in the "corporations" section of your state's secretary of state website. A list of the secretary of state departments that handle LLCs and corporations in each state can be found below.

Two main documents normally are filed when establishing an LLC. One is an operating agreement, which addresses the management and structure of the business, the distribution of profit and loss, the method of voting, and how changes in the organizational structure will be handled. The operating agreement is not required by every state.

Articles of Organization, however, are required by every state, and the required form is generally available for download from your state's website. The purpose of the Articles of Organization is to establish your business legally by registering with your state. It must contain, at a minimum, the following information:

- The limited liability company's name and the address of the principal place of business
- The purpose of the LLC
- The name and address of the LLC's registered agent (the person authorized to physically accept delivery of legal documents for the company)
- The name of the manager or managing members of the company
- An effective date for the company and signature

An example of the Articles of Organization for an LLC in Florida can be found on the companion CD.

Business Entity Chart

Legal entity	Costs involved	Number of owners	Paperwork	Tax implications	Liability issues
Sole proprietorship	Local fees assessed for registering business; generally between $25 and $100	One	Local licenses and registrations; fictitious name registration	Owner is responsible for all personal and business taxes.	Owner is personally liable for all financial and legal transactions.
Partnership	Local fees assessed for registering business; generally between $25 and $100	Two or more	Partnership agreement	Business income passes through to partners and is taxed at the individual level only.	Partners are personally liable for all financial and legal transactions, including those of the other partners.
LLC	Filing fees for articles of incorporation generally between $100 and $800, depending on the state	One or more	Articles of Organization; operating agreement	Business income passes through to owners and is taxed at the individual level only.	Owners are protected from liability; company carries all liability regarding financial and legal transactions.
Corporation	Varies with each state, can range from $100 to $500.	One or more; must designate directors and officers	Articles of Incorporation to be filed with state; quarterly and annual report requirements; annual meeting reports	Corporation is taxed as a legal entity; income earned from business is taxed at individual level.	Owners are protected from liability; company carries all liability regarding financial and legal transactions.

Corporation

Corporations are the most formal type of legal business structure, as well as the most common form of business organization. A corporation can be established as public or private and is chartered under the laws of the state where it is headquartered. A public corporation is owned by its shareholders (also known as stockholders) and is public because anyone can buy stocks in the company through public stock exchanges. Shareholders own shares or stocks, which represent a financial interest in the company. Many corporations start out as individually owned businesses and grow to the point where they seek additional financing by offering shares for sale in the open market. The first offer of shares to the public is called an **initial public offering** (IPO). Selling shares of your company diminishes your control over it by giving decision-making power to stockholders (shareholders) and a board of directors. Control is exercised through regular board of director meetings and annual stockholders' meetings. Records must be kept to document decisions made by the board of directors. Small, closely held corporations can operate more informally, but recordkeeping cannot be eliminated. Officers of a corporation can be liable to stockholders for improper actions.

A private corporation is owned and managed by a few individuals who are normally involved in the day-to-day decision-making and operations of the company. If you own a relatively small business but still wish to run it as a corporation, a private corporation is the optimal legal structure because it allows you to stay closely involved in the operation and management. Even as your business grows, you can continue to operate as a private corporation. There is no rule that says a private corporation must change to a public corporation when it reaches a certain size.

Whether private or public, a corporation is a separate legal entity capable of entering into binding contracts and being held directly liable in any legal issues. Its finances are not directly tied to anyone's personal finances, and it is taxed completely separately from its owners. These are only some of the many advantages to operating your business in the form of a corporation.

A business may incorporate without an attorney, but legal advice is highly recommended. The corporate structure is usually the most complex and is more costly to organize than the other two business forms. Forming a corporation can be a lengthy process, and the legal paperwork can put a strain on your budget. In addition to the startup costs, there are ongoing maintenance costs, as well as legal and financial reporting not required of partnerships or sole proprietorships.

To legally establish your corporation, it must be registered with the state in which the business is created by filing Articles of Incorporation. Filing fees, information to be included, and its actual format vary from state to state.

Some information usually required for incorporation:

- Name of the corporation
- Address of the registered office
- Purpose of the corporation
- Duration of the corporation
- Number of shares the corporation will issue
- Duties of the board of directors
- Status of the shareholders, such as quantity of shares and responsibilities
- Stipulation for the dissolution of the corporation

- Names of the incorporator(s) of the organization

- Statement attesting to the accuracy of the information contained therein

- Signature line and date

State offices responsible for filing Articles of Incorporation

The name of the government office that provides services to businesses and corporations is different in every state. Here is a list by state of the appropriate office for filing Articles of Incorporation:

State	Name of Division Responsible for Filing Articles of Incorporation
Alabama	Corporations Division
Alaska	Corporations, Businesses, and Professional Licensing
Arizona	Corporation Commission
Arkansas	Business/Commercial Services
California	Business Portal
Colorado	Business Center
Connecticut	Commercial Recording Division
Delaware	Division of Corporations
Florida	Division of Corporations
Georgia	Corporations Division
Hawaii	Business Registration Division
Idaho	Business Entities Division
Illinois	Business Services Department
Indiana	Corporations Division
Iowa	Business Services Division
Kansas	Business Entities
Kentucky	Corporations
Louisiana	Corporations Section
Maine	Division of Corporations
Maryland	Secretary of State

Massachusetts	Corporations Division
Michigan	Business Portal
Minnesota	Business Services
Mississippi	Business Services
Missouri	Business Portal
Montana	Business Services
Nebraska	Business Services
Nevada	Commercial Recordings Division
New Hampshire	Corporation Division
New Jersey	Business Formation and Registration
New Mexico	Corporations Bureau
New York	Division of Corporations
North Carolina	Corporate Filings
North Dakota	Business Registrations
Ohio	Business Services
Oklahoma	Business Filing Department
Oregon	Corporation Division
Pennsylvania	Corporation Bureau
Rhode Island	Corporations Division
South Carolina	Business Filings
South Dakota	Corporations
Tennessee	Division of Business Services
Texas	Corporations Section
Utah	Division of Corporations and Commercial Code
Vermont	Corporations
Virginia	Business Information Center
West Virginia	Business Organizations
Washington	Corporations
Washington, D.C.	Corporations Division
Wisconsin	Corporations
Wyoming	Corporations Division

S corporation

An S corporation is a legal structure designed for small businesses ("S corporation" means "small business corporation"). Until the inception of the LLC, the S corporation was the only legal structure that afforded small business owners some form of limited liability protection from creditors yet provided the benefits of a partnership. An S corporation is taxed in much the same way as a partnership or sole proprietorship. Each year's profits and losses are passed through to the shareholders, who must report them on their personal income tax returns. According to the IRS, shareholders must pay taxes on the profits the business realized for that year in proportion to the percentage they own of the company's stock.

In order to organize as an S corporation and qualify as such under IRS regulations, a business must meet the following requirements:

- It cannot have more than 100 shareholders.

- Shareholders must be U.S. citizens or residents.

- All shareholders must approve operating under this structure.

- It must be able to meet requirements for an S corporation the entire year.

Additionally, Form 253, "Election of Small Business Corporation," must be filed with the IRS within the first 75 days of the corporation's fiscal year.

Electing to operate under S corporation status is not effective for every business. However, many employee-owned and family-owned companies over the years have benefited from it. In 1966, the S Corporation Association of America (**www.s-corp.org**) was established to lobby in Washington, D.C., on behalf of small- and family-owned businesses against too much taxation and government regulation. The association represents the 4.5 million owners of S corporations in the U.S.

Financial Statement Requirements and Disclosure at a Glance by Business Structure

Business Type	Regulatory Requirement	Management Requirement	Investor and Lender Requirement
Sole Proprietors	None	Generally rely on common accounting software and reports. Financial statements are not relied on and audited statements are rare.	Lenders normally limit loan sizes and rely on owner's income tax returns and other personal information when making loan decisions. Loans are backed by the sole proprietor's personal property, in addition to business assets.
Partnerships	None	May rely on common accounting software; may have an accounting firm compile financial statements if a particular need arises	Similar to the sole proprietor, except two or more partners provide personal resources to guarantee loans.
Private C-Corp	Generally none. Some states require annual disclosure of total assets and liabilities but not a full set of financial statements.	Typically the largest of the private business structures. Senior management uses financial statements to manage daily operations, to provide the board of directors with ability to oversee the entire company, to keep investors informed as a requirement of bylaws, and to obtain loans. Stock option programs may make audited statements a requirement in the process of valuing the company and establishing a stock price.	Lenders frequently require GAAP conforming audited financial statements and include covenants about the total amount a company can borrow from all sources against assets. Investors normally require unaudited quarterly statements and audited annual statements to track financial performance.

Private S-Corp	Generally none. Some states require annual disclosure of total assets and liabilities but not a full set of financial statements.	The need for financial statements is made at management discretion. Accounting software may or may not give adequate oversight of the business, and with up to 100 investors, the corporate bylaws may mandate annually audited statements.	Similar to private C-corps. Lenders frequently require annual audited statements depending on loan sizes and associated risk. Investors that do not actively manage the business may require statements to verify management is competent.
Private LLC	Generally, none. Some states require annual disclosure of total assets and liabilities but not a full set of financial statements.	Generally, the same as private S-corps, but there can be more investors influencing the need.	Generally, the same as private S-corps, but there can be more investors influencing the need.
Public C-Corp	All financial statements publicly disclosed as defined by the SEC. Includes annual audited and quarterly unaudited reports along with other requirements.	Management regularly relies on financial statements to guide decision-making. Extensive public analysis requires management thoroughly understand information behind the numbers and be able to explain significant changes. Board of directors determines the outside firm to conduct the annual audit.	Lender requirements are similar as those for private C-corps. Investors can obtain copies from the SEC EDGAR database and have an opportunity to ask questions of management at the annual shareholders meeting.

How to Obtain an Employer Identification Number

All employers, partnerships, and corporations must have an employer identification number (EIN), also known as a federal tax identification number. You must obtain your EIN from the IRS before you conduct any business transactions or hire any employees. The IRS uses the EIN to identify the tax accounts of employers, certain sole proprietorships, corporations, and partnerships. The EIN is used on all tax forms and other licenses. To obtain an EIN, fill out Form SS-4, which you can obtain from the IRS at **www.irs.gov/businesses/small**. Click "Small Business Forms and Publications" and then "Filing and Paying Business Taxes." *A copy of this form is included on the companion CD.* There is no charge. If you are in a hurry to get your number, you can get an EIN assigned to you by telephone at 800-829-4933.

A sole proprietor who does not have employees can use his or her Social Security number on tax forms instead of an EIN.

Selecting a Name for Your Business

You will save yourself time and trouble if you decide on your business name before you start applying for licenses and registrations. You can set up a sole proprietorship, obtain licenses, and operate a business using just your first and last name. If you use your own name, you can avoid the expense of registering a fictitious name with your state government. There are advantages and disadvantages to using your personal name for the business. When you share your name and identity with your company, you create a personal or family connection with clients and with your target market. You also use your personal reputation and community image to help build up your business. Remember, however, that your name will become familiar to the public — for example, your children's teachers and friends at school will immediately recognize who they are. You may also want to add words to your personal name to create a business name that reflects the type of services you offer.

In choosing a name for your business, think about what clients are looking for in a personal financial planner and what you want people to think about when they read your name on a sign or business card. You might want to incorporate words that evoke thoughts of prosperity, financial security, debt relief, and integrity. Do you want to appeal to a particular niche market? For divorce or special needs, for example, a name like "Resilience Financial Planning" suggests your company can help clients to overcome their difficulties. Your name should project reliability and professionalism. Before making a final decision, ask relatives and friends what they think about your name choices. Add LLC, Inc., or Co., after the name if your business registration requires it.

Avoid long names that may be hard to remember. Think of how the name will sound when you answer the phone and how it will look on a billboard or brochure. Choose a name that accurately reflects what your business does while distinguishing it from another financial planner using a similar name down the street.

Factors to consider in coming up with a name for your personal financial planning business:

- Is it unique?

- Is it clear? Does it say what you do?

- Could it be confused with another business or type of business?

- Does it suggest individual or group practice?

- Does it suggest a comfortable or corporate environment?

- Where will it fall in alphabetical listings?

- How could it be illustrated? Think of a logo design for your business.

Conduct a thorough search to confirm no one else is using the name in the area where you will be doing business. Start with the Yellow Pages and the Internet. Type the name into several Internet search engines including Google (**www.google.com**), Microsoft's Bing™ (**www.bing.com**), and DMOZ Open Directory Project (**http://search.dmoz.org**).

Before you can register your company name with the secretary of state's office in your state, you must prove no other business in that state is using the same name. Most of the state websites where you can submit a business name registration begin with a name search of all businesses registered in that state. Your local county clerk has a record of all the fictitious names (or assumed names) registered in your county.

Finally, check to see if your name, or something similar to it, is available as an Internet domain name. Your website will be an important marketing tool for your business; many potential clients will visit your website before they contact you or look up your website to learn more about your business when they see the name somewhere else. Make sure your website will be easy for them to find. You can search for available domain names on the InterNIC website: **http://internic.net/whois.html**.

As soon as you have decided on a name, claim it. If you are using it as the name of your corporation, file your incorporation documents as soon as possible. If you are a sole proprietorship or partnership, register it as an assumed name (fictitious name) with the office of the secretary of state in your state and locally with your county clerk.

Register your domain name immediately with an inexpensive registrar such as GoDaddy.com® (**www.godaddy.com**) or Network Solutions® (**www.networksolutions.com**), along with possible misspellings and obvious variations. Each domain name costs only $7 to $10 per year (some of the new suffixes cost more). When you set up your website, you can arrange for all of these domain names to redirect to your site. Be sure to renew your domain names on time or set up automatic renewals so you do not lose the investment you have made in your website later on.

If there is a possibility that someone else might copy your business name, begin putting the symbol TM (trademark, used to distinguish a product) or SM (service mark, used to distinguish a service) after your name wherever you use it. You do not have to register a trademark or service mark to use these symbols. You can officially register a service mark or trademark with the U.S. government for $325 — a small amount to pay for the assurance that no one else can legally use your name.

Registering your name

If the name you use to operate your business is different from the name you registered as a business entity (such as a corporation), you must file a Fictitious Name registration or a Doing Business As (DBA) registration. The agency with which the fictitious name or DBA name is filed varies from state to state. In some states, the registration is done with the city or county in which the company has its principal place of business. However, the majority requires the registration to be done with the state's secretary of state. The only states that specifically do not require any type of filing when conducting business under a different name are Alabama, Arizona, Kansas, Mississippi, New Mexico, and South Carolina. Washington, D.C., makes it optional, and Tennessee does not require such filing for sole proprietorships or general partnerships.

From now on, all your contracts and legal documents will read "Your personal name or partnership name, DBA (doing business as) your business name."

Designing a Logo for Your Business

Your company logo, like your name, is an important element of your branding and your marketing strategies. Your logo is a visual symbol that instantly identifies your services. Just like the words in a name, the colors and forms of a logo convey specific feelings and messages. A logo can be your company name or initials, a simple shape, or an elaborately designed symbol. Even if you have already designed your logo, it is a good idea to get a graphic designer to create it for you using illustration software, so you will have high-quality images to use in print and on websites. A professional artist will make sure your logo design is balanced and aesthetically pleasing. If you cannot afford to hire a professional, look for a student or a friend who has experience with graphic design software. Or do it yourself using the logo design tools on Guru Corporation's Logosnap. com (**www.logosnap.com**) or HP's Logomaker (**www.logomaker.com**).

Your logo will appear on business cards and letterhead stationery, reports for clients, on your website, and on all of your products.

Registering Your Business

You will have to register your business locally with the city or county that has jurisdiction over the area where your office is located, and you may be required to get certain licenses or permits. Failure to register your business correctly could result in fines or penalties. Every county has its own rules for business registration; contact the office of your local county clerk or look up the regulations on its website. If you are running your business out of your home, you may be required to purchase an occupational license that must be renewed every year. If you are using an assumed name for your business, make sure the correct name is listed on the registration.

You can use the SBA.gov's Business Licenses and Permits Search Tool online (**www.sba.gov/content/search-business-licenses-and-permits**) to get a listing of the federal, state, and local permits, licenses, and registrations you will need to operate your business.

Most states do not require a sole proprietorship to register if it is operating under the owner's personal name. Businesses with assumed, or fictitious names, however, must be registered with the state.

As discussed earlier in this chapter, a corporation must register by filing its Articles of Incorporation with the state. A public corporation is required to file an annual audited financial report and quarterly unaudited reports along with other documents such as notices of changes to the corporate structure. All of this information is made available to the public on the SEC EDGAR database (**www.sec.gov/edgar.shtml**). Detailed information

Chapter 3: Setting Up Your Business   83

about corporations whose shares are trading on a stock exchange is available on the stock exchange's website and investment websites.

Keep copies of all your licensing applications, registration documents, and official forms. You may be required to display your business licenses in a prominent place. Maintain a list of all your licenses and registrations, along with their renewal dates. Mark renewal dates on a calendar. Remember that you may need additional business licenses if you expand your business to include new activities or services, such as selling insurance.

Opening a Bank Account

If you are operating as a sole proprietorship, you are not required to have a separate business bank account. You might not want to pay the fees to maintain a separate business account until you have regular business income. As soon as your business grows to the point where your personal finances must be kept separate from your business finances, a business bank account is necessary. A partnership, LLC, or corporation should have a bank account in its name.

Before going into a bank to open a business account, compare fees and services for business bank accounts by phoning local banks or looking on their websites. Meet with a bank representative when you go to open a business checking account and inquire about the services available for businesses, such as online banking, business credit cards, and business lines of credit. (A line of credit account is an arrangement whereby the bank extends a specified amount of unsecured credit to the borrower.) Some banks occasionally offer cash in your account or other incentives to open a business account. When you speak to the bank's customer service representative, you might be able to secure additional services, such as free checks, advertised by the bank's competitors.

To establish a business checking account, most financial institutions will require a copy of the state's Certificate of Fictitious Name Filing or a business license that shows the name in which you are opening the account. To open a business checking account for a corporation, most banks will require a copy of the Articles of Incorporation, an affidavit attesting to the actual existence of the company and the employer identification number acquired from the IRS.

If you anticipate doing business globally, you might prefer a bank with a strong international department, such as Bank of America, Wachovia, Global Connect, or Regions Bank, that will be able to handle and process specialized transactions, such as foreign exchange payments. Look for speed in handling transactions, electronic banking, a strong but flexible credit policy, and a solid relationship with other financial institutions overseas.

Get a Post Office Box

Whether you are working from a temporary office at home or have a separate physical address for your business, it is a good idea to secure a post office box at your nearest post office. You can rent a P.O. box online at the U.S. Postal Service website (**www.USPS.com**). Look under "Products and Services" for "P.O. Boxes Online."

Having a post office box for your company helps keep your business correspondence separate from your personal correspondence. Most important, it will prevent you from having to reprint any business stationery should you ever relocate your office. Continuity in any business means stability.

Taxes

A corporation reports income and pays taxes as a separate legal entity. In all the other types of business organizations — S corporations, LLCs, partnerships, and sole proprietorships — each year's business income and expenses are "passed though" to the individual owners and reported on their personal income tax returns. All legitimate business expenses are deducted from business revenues, and the balance is reported as income on the owners' tax returns. If expenses exceed revenue, that amount is reported as a loss on tax returns. For that reason, you do not want to overlook any expense that legitimately could be deducted from your taxable income.

According to IRS Publication 535 (**www.irs.gov/publications/p535**), a business expense must be "ordinary and necessary" to be deductible. An ordinary expense is one that is common and accepted in your industry, for example, office supplies and licensing fees. A necessary expense is one that is helpful and appropriate for your trade or business, such as printing brochures to hand out at educational seminars. An expense does not have to be indispensable to be considered necessary. You may need the help of a tax accountant to determine which of your expenses qualify as "ordinary and necessary."

Certain expenses, such as the cost of goods sold, expenses associated with starting up your business, and the purchase of land, vehicles, and equipment, are not deductible and must be "capitalized" (classified as long-term investments rather than current business expenses) instead. The cost of these items can be recovered by deducting a specified percentage each year as depreciation, amortization, or depletion.

You can deduct expenses such as mileage when you use your personal vehicle for business, travel, interest on money borrowed for your business, office supplies, and entertaining clients. It is important to keep receipts and statements that document these expenses. Make a habit of keeping all your receipts for business-related purchases and filing them away for future reference.

When you run your business out of your home, you can also deduct a portion of your utility bills, mortgage interest, and home maintenance costs as business expenses. The amount you can deduct is determined by the percentage of your home that is completely dedicated to your business — the number of square feet you use for your office, studio, or storage space.

It is important to be aware of tax rules, so you can comply with them from the beginning and get the maximum tax deduction. Learn from other business owners and consult a tax accountant or lawyer.

Business expenses must be itemized on *IRS Schedule C* and filed with your *Federal Form 1040*. If you are self-employed, you probably will have to file a *Schedule SE*. According to *IRS Publication 533*, you must pay self-employment taxes (SE taxes) if your net earnings from self-employment activities were more than $400. SE tax is a Social Security and Medicare tax for individuals who work for themselves, similar to the Social Security and Medicare taxes withheld from the pay of most wage earners. A self-employed individual is required to file an annual return and pay estimated tax quarterly. Use the worksheet in IRS *Form 1040-ES, Estimated Tax for Individuals* (**www.irs.gov/pub/irs-pdf/f1040es.pdf**) to find out if you are required to file quarterly estimated tax. You may have to pay a penalty to the IRS if you fail to make quarterly estimated income tax payments.

The amount of SE tax you must pay each quarter is calculated based on the income reported in your income tax *Form 1040* from the previous year. If this is your first year being self-employed, you will need to estimate the amount of income you expect to earn for the year. Form 1040-ES contains blank vouchers you can use to mail in your estimated tax payments, or you can make your payments online using the Electronic Federal Tax Payment System (EFTPS). If you over-estimated your earnings for one quarter and paid too much tax, complete another Form 1040-ES worksheet to refigure your estimated tax for the next quarter. If your earnings estimate was too low, complete another *Form 1040-ES* worksheet to recalculate your estimated taxes for the next quarter. You can find more information on SE tax online at the Self-Employed Individuals Tax Center (**www.irs.gov/ businesses/small/article/0,,id=115045,00.html#obligations**).

Each time you hire a new employee, he or she must fill out an IRS *Form W-4, "Employer Withholding Allowance Certificate."* The Form W-4 determines how much income tax, Social Security, and Medicare tax is withheld from each paycheck. The frequency with which you have to deposit these withheld taxes with the IRS is determined by the amount of taxes you reported for your company two years previously (the look-back period). Payroll software automatically calculates withheld taxes when it prints paychecks. You can find more information in *IRS Publication (Circular E), Employer's Tax Guide* (**www.irs.gov/pub/irs-pdf/p15.pdf**).

When you hire someone, such as an accountant, to do occasional work for you or to do "work for hire" (work on a one-time project), that person is treated as an independent contractor, and you do not have to withhold taxes on his or her behalf. Payments to an independent contractor that total $600 or more for the tax year must be reported to the IRS on *Form 1099-MISC, "Miscellaneous Income,"* and a copy must be given to the independent contractor. The independent contractor is responsible for paying his or her own income and SE taxes to the IRS. If you are uncertain about how to treat temporary workers for tax purposes, read "Independent Contractor (Self-Employed) or Employee?" on the IRS website (**www.irs.gov/businesses/small/article/0,,id=99921,00.html**) or consult a tax accountant or lawyer.

Purchasing a Business

One way to get started as an independent personal financial planner is to buy an existing business from someone else. If you buy a personal financial planning business, you will be associated with a known business model — that of the previous owner. This may or may not be a good thing, depending on the seller and how he or she operated the business. When you purchase a financial planning business, you are acquiring a customer list, some equipment, a reputation, and possibly an ongoing contract or two.

In theory, you will be buying a business that is already producing income instead of having to wait for several months or years before you secure enough clients to bring in cash. The price of the business is a primary consideration. How much can you afford to spend, and what are you getting for your money? Scrutinize the business's financial statements from the last two or three years, and have a lawyer and an accountant review them for any potential red flags or legal problems.

A client's decision to do business with a particular financial planner is largely based on the personal connection. When you buy a business, the existing clients may not feel as comfortable working with you as they did with the previous owner. Purchasing an existing financial planning business gives you a good starting point, but it does not ensure success. If possible, ask the departing owner to introduce you personally to each client, and offer reassurance that they will receive the same level of attention and service. If the previous owner is deceased or unavailable, send out letters, make personal phone calls, and arrange a meeting with each client to review his or her accounts and establish a relationship between you. Remember that new business often comes through referrals from existing clients. Although you might lose a few existing clients, you may be able to instill even greater confidence in others who will recommend you to their friends and relatives.

A "non-compete" clause in the sale contract legally prohibits the seller of the business from taking existing clients from the business you just bought and setting up another financial planning business. Some non-compete clauses stipulate a period when the seller cannot perform duties as a financial planner. Other non-compete clauses specify a geographic area in which the seller cannot perform duties related to financial planning, such as within five miles of the existing business. Before you sign the sale contract, consider your future relationship with the seller of the financial planning business, and make sure any conditions or restrictions are spelled out in the contract.

Working for Someone Else

If you feel buying a new business or starting from scratch is more than you want to take on, you can look for an opportunity to join a firm that already offers personal financial planning. Another option is to join a company with an existing team of finance professionals (such as an estate attorney and a CPA) that wants to add a personal financial planner. You can receive training from your more experienced colleagues and postpone starting your own business until you feel confident to work on your own.

CASE STUDY: PAVING THE PATH TO COLLEGE EDUCATIONS

Felicia Gopaul, CFP
College Funding Resource
590 Bloomfield Avenue #238
Bloomfield, NJ 07003
www.collegefundingresource.com
feliciag@collegeplanningresource.com

In the beginning of her practice, Felicia Gopaul primarily worked with parents of young children who were interested in saving for their children's future college education, but she also kept running into parents of high school students who were concerned about the high cost of college right around the corner. Possible solutions included taking money from retirement plans, incurring additional debt, or suggesting that their children consider "less expensive" colleges. After seeing the disappointment on the faces of a family after she told the parents of a high school senior it was too late to save enough to pay for college, Gopaul decided to educate herself on financial aid rules and regulations to see if something could be done. Her research showed a big gap between getting into college and graduating from college — the difference was often related to whether the student's family had the necessary money.

Every year, more than 2.5 million students graduate from high school nationally, and Gopaul found that middle- to high-income families tend to have a problem. The incomes and the assets they have worked a lifetime to gather can keep them from getting the financial aid they need. This did not seem fair to Gopaul. It is almost like these parents are being penalized for doing the right thing: saving and investing for their kids' education, Gopaul thought.

Parents often invested significant time and money in "financial aid nights," Internet research, scholarship books, tutors, and test preparation courses. However, these activities may not be particularly helpful to their kids in putting together strategies for paying for college. Even after doing their own research, parents often are left with the idea that their only options for paying for college are scholarships, grants, and student loans. That is because college-funding information is often limited to explanations of various government programs, scholarship sources, and student loan information. To make things worse, this information is scattered among various sources, so it can require a lot of work to find, process, and apply it to a personal situation.

At College Funding Resource, which Gopaul founded, the fundamental belief is that learning more about the various college funding options in advance can save time, money, and frustration for parents of college-bound kids. Because out-of-the-area parents cannot attend Gopaul's seminars and events, she has put together a brain trust of college-planning experts, articles, videos, and other resources to cut through the clutter of available information and directly deliver the practical knowledge parents need to make informed choices.

Gopaul said she grew up in a household that emphasized the importance of getting a college education. When she realized that her financial planning training to date was not preparing her to help families who were in the later stages of college planning, she learned about the NICCP (National Institute of Certified College Planners) and became a member. The institute teaches certified advisers how to help families of all income levels plan for college, even when their student does not qualify for financial aid.

Gopaul is a Certified Financial Planner professional and a Certified College Planning Specialist — one of fewer than 500 people in the United States with that designation. In addition, she is the president of College Funding Resource and the creator of the CollegeExpertsTalk product and system, which helps educate families on how to make college an affordable reality without jeopardizing the family's retirement and other financial priorities.

CHAPTER 4

Writing a Business Plan

The old saying, "if you fail to plan, you plan to fail," is particularly applicable to starting a business. As a financial planner and adviser, you already have the skills and resources to produce an excellent written business plan. A good business plan serves several important functions. It is a thorough assessment of what you want to accomplish, how you plan to go about it, and what your financial resources are. Creating a written business plan helps you to develop and think through your ideas and foresee all eventualities. You are forced to consider every aspect of your new business, including how much you will spend to establish and operate it, assets and skills you can contribute to the business, sales and profit expectations, strategies for expanding the business, and how you will exit the business. A business plan is also your sales pitch to prospective investors and business partners, lenders from whom you wish to borrow money for the business, and suppliers from whom you want to buy on credit. A well-crafted business plan shows you understand your business thoroughly and are planning for the future. Finally, a business plan serves as a yardstick to measure your progress and help you adjust your goals and expectations as the business grows.

During the process of writing your business plan, you will gather all of your financial data in one place, along with business research, legal documents such as rental agreements and contracts, and any other information important to your business. You will be forced to look at details, add up the figures, and see where you might have overlooked expenses and where you might be able to cut down costs. The more effort you invest in writing your business plan, the more useful it will be.

Writing a complete business plan takes a lot of thought, research, and preparation. There are numerous books on the subject, software programs, and even professional business plan writers, but because you are starting a small business with few physical assets, you should be able to write your own plan. Start by writing down the answers to the following questions:

- Is there a local, regional, or industry need for the type of planning you wish to provide?

- Is there a niche your business will be able to serve?

  - Do the financial planning services you plan to offer fill this niche?

- Is there an adequate market for your financial planning business to turn a sufficient profit?

  - Is there too much competition, or will it be too expensive to advertise to attract enough customers?

  - Will your customers be able to pay for the services you are offering?

- What differentiates your financial planning business from your competition?

  - What does your business offer a client that is better or different from your competition?
  - Do you have enough qualified employees to provide this service?

- Will you be readily available to your customers?

- If your financial planning business caters to a specific geographic location, will it be centrally located to benefit your customers?

  - Is the location affordable?

- Do you have the skills and resources available to serve your customers?

  - What materials and products do you require to serve your customer needs?

A typical business plan is between 10 and 30 pages long, but yours may be shorter in the beginning. Save your business plan on your computer, and keep a paper copy in a file or binder. As your business grows, add copies of important documents such as partnership agreements, contracts, budgets, lists of prospective clients, marketing strategies, and contact information for vendors, companies, and individuals who provide you with services. From time to time, review and update your business plan to reflect your current circumstances. Your business plan can help you make important decisions based on whether they fit in with your original business ideas and get back on track when your business starts to deviate from your original expectations. Either you will refocus your business activities or alter your business plan to incorporate the new direction you are taking. When you seek additional financing or take on a new partner, your business plan can be rewritten in a more professional manner with the help of business plan software or books to present a clear picture of your business to your prospective partners.

Elements of a Business Plan

A business plan is made up of four main elements:

1. **Company description:** A complete description of your company and the services it offers to your clients

2. **Marketing plan:** An outline of the activities you will do to advertise your planning business and attract customers

3. **Business structure:** A detailed explanation of how you plan to structure and manage your business

4. **Financials:** A detailed outline of the expected startup and operating costs for your personal financial planning business and a description of how you will manage these expenses

A business plan is always a work in progress. In the beginning, you need a business plan to obtain necessary financing and to launch your financial planning business. Throughout your first year of business, your business plan will evolve as you work with your clients and learn from your experiences. Your short- and long-term goals for your business, and your marketing plan and financial projections, may change. You will add more sections when you apply for a loan, add a new business partner, file your first tax returns, or sign a lease for a new office.

Basic outline for a business plan

I.   Cover sheet

II. Statement of purpose

III. Table of contents

IV. Mission statement

V. Executive summary

VI. The business

    1. Description of business

        a) Industry background

        b) Product description

    2. Marketing analysis

        a) Target market

        b) Product description

        c) Market approach strategy

        d) Competition

        e) Strengths and weaknesses

    3. Personnel — management and staffing

        a) Résumés, strengths

        b) Roles and responsibilities

        c) Operating procedures

    4. Financial management

        a) Capital, assets

        b) Accounting system

        c) Financing, loan applications

        d) Payment of principals and employees

        e) Business Insurance

VII. Financial data (you will add to this section as your business progresses)

a) Balance sheet

b) Break-even analysis

c) Pro forma income projections

    1. Three-year summary

    2. Detail by month for the first year in business

d) Detail by quarter for the second and third years in business

e) Pro forma cash flow statements

VIII. Supporting documents

    a) Tax returns of principals for the last three years

    b) Personal financial statement

    c) In the case of a franchised business, a copy of the franchise contract and all supporting documents provided by the franchisor

    d) Copy of proposed lease or purchase agreement for building space

    e) Copies of licenses and other legal documents

    f) Copies of résumés of all principals

    g) Copies of letters of intent from suppliers and vendors

Cover page

Think of the cover page as your chance to make a good first impression. The cover page sets the tone for what the reader can expect from the rest of the document. It should be laid out evenly with all the information centered on the page. Always write the name of your company in all capital letters in the upper half of the page. Several line spaces down, write the title "Business Plan." A cover page should include your business logo, the date the document was created, your name as the owner of the company, the business address, telephone number, e-mail address, and website address.

NAME OF COMPANY

Business Plan

Address
Contact Name
Date

Statement of purpose

This section contains one to three paragraphs explaining the purpose of your business plan and may be altered to suit different purposes. A statement of purpose for an initial business plan explains why you are starting the business and what you hope to accomplish, while a business plan submitted with a loan application would explain (briefly) why you are applying for the loan and how the money will be used.

Your mission statement

A mission statement is a well-written paragraph (sometimes two paragraphs) stating the purpose of your business, the products and services you provide, and something about your company's attitude towards its employees and customers. If written and advertised correctly, your mission statement can become a valuable marketing tool by helping to shape your public image. It will also set the tone for your company's internal policies, help you to affirm your purpose, and guide your business in the direction you want it to go.

To create a mission statement, list your top priorities and discuss them with your business associates, friends, and family to see how they react. Try to explain why these priorities are important to you. Think about what you want to do with your business, such as helping retirees manage their incomes and plan their estates or assisting young couples plan for their families. Consider the qualities you are trying to convey to your clients, such as integrity, stability, and prosperity. Experiment with words and phrases until you have created a statement that is clear and understandable. Try to keep it simple and avoid clichés or vague language. A good mission statement will serve as a reminder of your original intentions for your business.

Many companies put all or part of their mission statements on the "About Us" sections of their websites. Reading the mission statements of companies similar to yours will give you an idea of what you might or might not want to include in your own statement.

Executive summary

The executive summary is a summary of the information in your business plan and should be about one to two pages long. It should be written after you have completed the rest of your business plan. The executive summary contains essential information about your business, such as your target market, how the business will be managed, the expertise of your staff, the products and services you offer, and how you plan to advertise to prospective clients. Write the executive summary to prompt the reader to look deeper into the business plan. It is a good idea to discuss the various elements of your business plan in the order you address them in the rest of the document.

Body of the business plan

The body of the business plan describes in detail how your business will operate and make money and how it will achieve the goals set forth in your mission statement. It can be divided into four distinct sections:

1. A description of the business

Your business description should explain the type of financial planning services you will provide, the legal structure of the business, whether the business is new or you are taking over an existing company, the name of the business and the owners, and specific and measurable goals for the business. It should include an overview of the financial planning industry in your area with available facts, figures, and examples of similar businesses that have recently experienced success. Identify your competition and explain what sets your company apart from others in the same field. The information in this section should inspire you (and your future clients, investors, partners, and lenders) to believe your company will be taking advantage of an excellent business opportunity. It should also prepare you to answer any questions you may be asked during a presentation or sales pitch with confidence and self-assurance.

2. Marketing analysis

The marketing plan should be one of the most comprehensive sections of your business plan and can be several pages long depending on the number of products involved and the market you intend to cover.

The marketing analysis will require you to gather data on the specialty you have chosen and on the demographics of the area where your business will be located. Trade journals that cater to financial planners and stockbrokers are helpful resources for this type of information. You will find demographic data on the websites of the U.S. Bureau of Labor Statistics (**www.bls.gov**) and the U.S. Census Bureau (**www.census.gov**).

The market analysis contains:

- The niche you are targeting

- The current state of the niche (stable, growing, or declining)

- The future of the niche

- The demographics of your current and potential customers

- The size of your potential market

- The estimated dollar value of the segment of the market that is potential business for you

Marketing plan

This section of the business plan describes in detail your advertising and public relations strategies for making potential clients aware of your business. You may offer the best financial planning services in the country, but if no one knows you exist, you will not make any sales. *Read more about developing and implementing a strategic marketing plan in Chapter 8.*

The marketing plan includes:

- A description of your target audience(s)

- The menu of services along with the pricing

- The types of the marketing and advertising you will use to build your brand, grab the attention of your target market, and convert them into customers

Describe, in detail, the strategies you intend to employ to reach your target market. For example, you might plan to offer financial education at luncheon seminars in local restaurants and churches, and send out postcards to all the homeowners in a designated area. Discuss major changes that have taken place in the industry in the recent past, which will affect how you will conduct business. Estimate the cost of implementing various marketing strategies. This should include the cost of setting up and maintaining a website, purchasing advertising on the Internet and radio, printing brochures and postcards, and memberships to local professional organizations.

Based on demographics and industry statistics, estimate how much revenue you can expect to receive from your services and/or sales of your products.

Marketing plan software

Get help writing a detailed marketing plan with software that walks you through the process. You can download a free template for creating a marketing plan in Microsoft® Office from the Microsoft Startup Center website (**www.microsoft.com/smallbusiness/ startup-toolkit/marketing-plan-for-startups.aspx**). Palo Alto Software (**www.paloalto.com**) offers free sample marketing plans on its Mplans website (**www.mplans.com**), along with its marketing plan software. Other companies selling marketing plan software include Business Resources Software (**www.brs-inc.com/marketing_plan.asp**) and Planware (**www.planware.org/salepwm.htm**).

3. Competition analysis

The next area of the business plan is a review and analysis of your competition. You can learn a lot by observing what your competition is (and is not) doing. You first need to identify who your competitors are. Then, you need to conduct an in-depth analysis of their business operations. Answer the following questions about your competition:

- What areas (in terms of geography, industry, and niche markets) does your competition serve?

- How does your financial planning business differ from that of your competition?

- How do your competitors price their services, and how does this compare to your pricing?

- How experienced are your competitors, and how does your level of experience compare?

- Do your competitors have strong name recognition within your target market, and how much market share does each competitor have?

- Are your competitors growing, declining, or stable?

- Why would a customer choose you over your competition? What is your unique selling proposition (USP)?

- What is your competition doing to market its services? What is and is not working?

- What are the strengths and weaknesses of your competition and what are your own?

4. Strengths and weaknesses

Finally, evaluate the strengths and weaknesses of your business. Your strengths are anything that gives your company a market advantage. Strengths might include your knowledge and experience as a financial planner, an existing client base, relationships or partnerships with businesses or individuals who can help you break into the market, and your intuitive grasp of a particular niche market. Your skills and those of your partners or employees are also strengths. You might have special licenses or certifications, years of experience in estate planning or insurance sales, or advanced computer skills that will allow you to respond quickly to new opportunities. Weaknesses could include inexperience or lack of knowledge about important aspects of your business, such as reporting software, accounting, foreclosure law, or life insurance. Limited financial resources are also a weakness because they restrict your ability to market on a large scale. Explain how you will employ each strength to the maximum advantage of your business. Describe what you are doing to correct or compensate for each weakness.

Additional sections

Personnel — management and staffing

In this section, give a brief résumé for each of the principals in your business (a principal is an owner, partner, or executive who makes business and policy decisions for a company). Emphasize the qualities and experiences each person contributes to your business. Outline the role and responsibility of each principal. If you will be operating your business alone, explain which aspects of the business you will handle yourself and which you will "outsource" to other individuals or companies. Include a brief description of other staff members and their responsibilities.

Describe how decisions are made in your company, who makes them, and how they are put into practice. If your business is already operating, outline how each person carries out his or her responsibilities — for example, the procedure followed when a new client comes into your office. Discuss how financial plans are presented and what happens when you take a client's assets under your management.

This is also where you should mention any labor policies, such as a drug-free workplace, retirement savings plans, and health benefits for employees.

Are you a good business manager?

If you have always worked for someone else, you may not have experience running a business. In addition to managing your own work, you will now have to handle business finances and give direction to other employees. Your ability to manage your business will ultimately define its success.

Ask yourself the following questions:

- Do you have the background and the experience to run a successful financial planning business?

- What are your shortcomings related to running a business, and how will you compensate for those shortcomings?

- Which employees, if any, will you need to add to your management team?

- How will your employees' strengths and weaknesses complement your shortcomings?

- What tasks will you assign to each member of the team?

- How will you outline your employees' responsibilities?

- What amount of help do you need to get your business started?

- How will you hire and train employees to be part of your team?

- What salary and benefits will you provide to each team member?

Instead of struggling to do everything yourself, you can hire, at least on a part-time basis, someone who has the skills you lack and free yourself to spend time with your clients. For example, an office manager can help you with scheduling and billing, someone with computer skills can set up your software programs and help you produce reports, or an accounting service can take care of sending out monthly statements and processing payments.

Do not let a lack of knowledge or experience sabotage your new business. Learn management skills by taking a class, reading a book, or working with a business coach.

The U.S. Small Business Administration provides small business counseling and training through district offices across the country and on its website (**www.sba.gov**). SCORE (Service Corps of Retired Executives) (**www.score.org**), a partner of the U.S. Small Business Administration, provides free business coaching and mentorship programs online and through its 364 chapters. Coaching and mentorship programs also are available through many local Chambers of Commerce (**www.uschamber.com**) and professional associations. Professional small business coaches charge fees but promise to help you get your business up and running in record time. Find a small business coach in your area by searching online.

Financial management

This section should begin with a list of your capital and assets (business capital, assets under management, existing clients, equipment, vehicles, real estate) as well as major financial liabilities (debts, rental contracts, necessary expenses). Because financial planning is primarily a service industry, many independent financial planners start out with little capital and expand their operations as their business grows. Include income projections for the next year and the next three years.

Describe your accounting system, who will do your bookkeeping, and how income and expenses will be documented. Explain how principals and employees will be paid: hourly wages, fixed salaries, or a percentage of income. Outline policies for expense accounts or spending limits for business expenses. The more detail you can give in this section, the more clearly you will be able to understand the financial situation of your business later on.

Identify possible sources of financing and how this financing might be secured if the need arises. It is also a good idea to establish an exit plan, a strategy to close your business and cut your losses if you fail to make a profit for an extended period. This can be as simple as saying, "If I am not making a profit in two years, I will close the business." When partners or investors are involved, they should agree on specific indicators that will trigger a financial review of the business, such as repeated failures to meet monthly sales targets.

Describe the insurance policies held by your business, the coverage they offer, and the cost of insurance premiums. *See the reference to life insurance in the section on Partnerships in Chapter 3.*

Business Insurance

Business insurance protects businesses from financial losses due to events that may occur during the normal course of business. A disgruntled client could file a lawsuit against you for a mistake, actual or perceived, in handling his or her financial affairs or try to hold you legally responsible for financial losses. A client or employee could slip and fall on your premises and sue you for damages. Even if you are not liable, legal expenses could send you into bankruptcy. Insurance is a necessary expense; it protects you from risk and guarantees you will not have to close your business because of misfortune.

A small home office may be covered under a homeowner's insurance policy. Take pictures, create an itemized list of your equipment, and keep an updated record of models, serial numbers, and receipts. A copy of this record should be on file with your insurance agent. Your insurance company may suggest purchasing additional insurance if the value of your equipment exceeds that of normal home electronics systems.

Startup budget

Startup costs are one-time expenses necessary to get your business up and running. Your main expenses will be fees for licenses, registrations, and legal assistance, the cost of renting and furnishing an office, and advertising to attract your first customers. Chapter 1 explained that a new financial planning business would not begin paying for itself right away; you will need enough money to support the business and pay for your living expenses until the business is established. Your startup costs will be higher if you are establishing a corporation or are taking over an existing business.

Sample Startup Expenses
for a Financial Planner

Computer equipment	Amount
Computer upgrade (or purchase)	
Software	
Scanner	
Copier	
Fax machine	
Printer	
Laptops	
Blackberry, iPad, PDA, etc.	
Calculators	
Office furniture and supplies	
Large file cabinet	
New phone	
Letterhead stationery	
Desk and chair	
Seating for clients, furnishings for reception area	
Office supplies	
Head set	
Business expenditures	
Office lease	
Legal advice	
Local business license	
Utility deposits	
Cell phone service	
Certifications	
Memberships to local professional associations	
Internet service	

Registration with SEC, licenses	
Marketing	
Business cards	
Advertising in local papers	
Internet advertising	
Radio	
Postcards and direct mail	
TOTAL	

1. Balance sheet

   A balance sheet is like a snapshot of a business's financial condition at a given point in time, such as the last day of its financial year. It usually has three sections: a list of assets and their values, a list of liabilities, and ownership equity. Assets are everything the company owns, including cash, physical property, inventory such as unsold CDs and merchandise, and intangible assets such as copyrights and contracts. Liabilities are the business's financial obligations, including unpaid bills, taxes, and loans. Ownership equity is the difference between total assets and total liabilities. Good-quality accounting software, if it is set up correctly, can provide you with an up-to-date balance sheet anytime you need it.

2. Break-even analysis

   A break-even analysis is a calculation of the amount of sales volume needed to cover operating costs and pay off your startup expenses. When sales volume exceeds that amount, your business will make a profit. If sales volume is lower than that amount, you will lose money. A break-even analysis helps you to set realistic goals for your business and to decide how much you can afford to spend on setup and marketing. For example, your business must bring in enough cash to justify the expense of renting an office in an upscale neighborhood.

3. Pro forma income projections (profit and loss statements)

    A pro forma income projection is an estimate of the company's expected revenues for a future period, based on market prices, the cost of goods and services, and allowances for loss.

    a. Three-year summary
    b. Detail by month, first year
    c. Detail by quarters, second and third years
    d. Assumptions upon which projections were based

4. Pro forma cash flow (Include same points as for number 3 above.)

    A pro forma cash flow is a picture of what your company's cash flow should look like over a certain period. It shows all the cash coming into your business, including your contributions and money from loans or investors as well as revenue from sales, and all the money that will be paid out over the period, including rent, payments to employees, and loan repayments.

An accountant can help with your financial projections

An accountant can give you a second or objective opinion on the financial estimates for your business, provide advice, review your research, and formulate reports about your organization to help refine your plan. Gather your preliminary costs, facts, and figures before seeking the advice of an accountant, so he or she can review the numbers with you and make sure they are realistic.

Operating budget

Your operating budget is the amount of money needed to keep your business running. It includes the cost of rent, phone, lights, and Internet service; wages of any employees; gas and maintenance of your vehicle; renewals of licenses and registrations; and the cost of marketing and advertising. If you are running your financial planning business out of a home office, your operating budget and expenses will be much lower than if you are renting office space.

Prepare a budget by researching the current prices of goods and services. If you lease an office space, contact the previous tenant to obtain an estimate of the monthly utility bill. Look up the prices of equipment, stationery, and office supplies in stores and catalogs (most of this research can be done online) and confirm the amounts of registration fees. *The CD-ROM accompanying this book contains a worksheet that can serve as a guideline.*

When you create your operating budget, set aside an amount equal to 25 or 30 percent of your total expenses to cover unexpected costs and emergencies, such as unanticipated repairs to a vehicle or a computer. This financial cushion will allow your business to continue operating smoothly instead of going into crisis mode when something unexpected happens. Revisit your operating budget from time to time and adjust it based on your actual expenses. If you anticipate you will not have enough money to continue operating until you begin to realize a profit, look for ways to cut costs or take out a loan.

There many variables involved in generating the estimates and projected figures for your business, and consequently, there is no set formula for coming up with these numbers. One way to get an idea of projected figures is to look at sample financial planning business plans. One online resource for sample business plans is B Plans (**www.bplans.com**). Again, your fee schedules and service offering would have to be identical in order to project the same figures as the sample, but the sample can be used as a guide.

Supporting documents

Supporting documents are legal documents providing concrete evidence that the other sections of your business plan are accurate. This includes rental property leases, agreements with companies whose products you sell, contracts with clients, insurance policies, and any other document that contains important information pertaining to your company. By looking at these documents, a prospective lender or investor can see what you are saying about your business is true. Personal information about you and your partners, such as copies of previous tax returns, résumés, and personal financial statements, shows you are qualified to run a successful business and that your financial liabilities will not cripple the company. By looking at your tax returns, a loan officer can see how much you have been earning from the business in recent years. Supporting documents include:

1. Tax returns of principal officers for the last three years

2. Personal financial statement(s) (all banks have these forms)

3. Copy of proposed lease or purchase agreement for office

4. Copy of licenses and other legal documents.

5. Copy of résumés of all principal officers

6. Copies of contracts with clients; agreements with brokerages, insurance providers, and other companies whose products you sell.

Sample Business Plan

Resilience Financial Planning
Business Plan
Sept. 29, 2009

Mission: Resilience Financial Planning offers responsible personal financial planning services and investment products to individuals and families in the seaside region of Alaska.

Values: Resilience strives to uphold fairness, compassion, and integrity

Executive summary

Resilience Financial Planning is a personal financial planning firm offering a modest array of services to residents of Seaside, Alaska. The operation, a sole proprietorship founded by Paige Stanley, CFP, MBA, is operated year-round from her home at 4012 Seaside Drive in Seaside. Resilience offers standard financial planning services. Its initial target market is individuals, couples, and families aged 20 to 60 with incomes from $40,000 or higher. Resilience will sell AK-World insurance products in 2010, its first full year of operation, and plans to add AK-World investment products by January 2011. Stanley is evaluating a small retail space in the Whittier Strip Mall for relocation in 2012.

Market analysis

Seaside is a city of 4,024 residents located on the Kenai Peninsula in Alaska, several hours by car from Anchorage. Recent annual population growth was 15.2 percent. The median age is 34 and the median income $52,985. Major industries include fishing, tourism, and retail trade. A branch of the University of Alaska in town employs eight people full-time, with 28 adjuncts.

The Resilience service area has experienced strong, sustained growth in population and property values over the past decade, even during recent setbacks in the real estate industry nationally. During the recent economic downturn, the Alaskan economy has fared better than many states in the lower 48.

Company description

Resilience is a sole proprietorship formed in March 2009 by Paige Stanley. Stanley, who graduated in May 2008 from the University of Anchorage with an MBA in marketing, attained the Certified Financial Planner (CFP) credential online (see attachment) in July 2004. She holds a bachelor's degree in urban planning from UA-Fairbanks. The year 2010 will mark the first full year of operation for Resilience, which operates under a State of Alaska business license as a personal financial planning business.

Organization and management

In the first full year of operation, Paige Stanley, who works 50 hours a week at the business, will manage Resilience Financial Planning. She expects to be joined in the business within two years by her brother, Scott

Stanley, who expects to relocate to Seaside from Seattle by February 2011. Scott Stanley has a bachelor's degree in engineering.

Paige Stanley is proposing to hire a part-time receptionist/recruiter in June 2010, who would work up to 20 hours a week, from 9 a.m. to noon Monday through Thursday and 9 a.m. to 5 p.m. on Friday.

Marketing and sales management

Paige Stanley intends to add two independent contractors to work on commission as sales recruiters by the end of 2010.

Resilience advertises mainly through weekly $50 display ads, placed and approved by Paige Stanley, in the *Seaside Gazetteer*. In anticipation of the new year, Resilience will distribute fliers at each home in the target area once a week for four weeks in December 2009; approximately 4,000 fliers total. Each home will receive the flier at least twice. To follow the flier up, Stanley will have a table at the January Fest answering personal financial planning and some basic investment questions. Stanley will also pass out business cards at the January Fest.

Services and products

Resilience Financial Planning offers basic services to clients seeking help with personal financial planning, at this time primarily in the areas of debt management, education, retirement, and estate planning. Currently, Stanley refers customers seeking insurance or investment products to AK-World of Anchorage's satellite office on Pioneer Place in Seaside.

By the latter half of 2011, Resilience intends to begin selling AK-World insurance products directly and plans to add direct AK-World investment options by January 2012. Working through AK-World's training program in Seattle and Anchorage, Scott Stanley is attaining required insurance and securities licenses to manage insurance and investments directly for Resilience.

Preliminary financials — completed two-year figures, including startup costs, to be submitted by June 2010

These figures are projections at this time

Service	2009*	2010*	2011*
General financial planning	$42,000	$45,000	$48,500
Divorce financial planning	$7,000	$10,000	$13,000
Costs			
Computer	$2,900	$3,000	$4,000
Phone	$2,000	$2,525	$2,790
Insurance/licensing/legal	$2,800	$3,100	$3,500
Marketing	$4,000	$4,000	$6,000
Fuel	$1,800	$2,500	$2,200

List here what you anticipate the cost of opening your personal financial planning business will be:

Funding requests — pending

CHAPTER 5

Financing and Insuring Your Business

A financial planning business does not require as much startup capital as some types of businesses, such as factories, restaurants, or retail stores, because you do not have to buy machinery, goods, raw materials, and store furnishings. You can meet with your clients in a small office, and you probably already own the computer and some of the software you will need to get started. On the other hand, you will not begin making money as soon as you open your doors. You will need to support yourself (and your family) and pay your operating expenses for six to eighteen months before you see a profit. If you do not have enough savings to carry you through this period, you will need to procure a loan or find other sources of income.

The type of services you offer and the business model you intend to follow will determine your startup costs. If you are going to sell securities or insurance, you will have to pay licensing fees and buy additional business insurance. To impress wealthy clients, you will need a prestigious, well-furnished office; if you are only charging a fee to prepare personal financial plans, you can meet with clients in their homes or in your home office.

Conventional small business loans from banks have been especially difficult to obtain since the recession that began in 2007. Banks are reluctant to approve loans. You must have an excellent credit history, provide assurance that you can and will pay back the loan, and offer some form of collateral such as savings, investments, your home, or other real estate property. If you cannot obtain a conventional loan, you will have to be creative in finding other ways to fund your business.

Investors and lenders expect you to provide a significant amount of the capital necessary to launch or expand your business. When you put your assets on the line, it demonstrates you are committed to making the company a success and makes it easier for you to acquire supplemental funding.

Ways to finance a personal financial planning business

- **Give it** — The primary source for business financing comes from personal savings.

- **Borrow it** — Commercial, government, or private loans range from small business seed money to multimillion-dollar open lines of credit.

- **Sell it** — Sell a part of your company to investors who can provide needed capital, but shared ownership has its drawbacks.

- **Earn it** — Save additional funds until you have enough money to fund the startup, maintenance, and growth of the business.

- **Pledge it** — Private or public business development grants are available based upon your ability and willingness to "give back" to the community.

- **Share it** — Find an up-line sponsor (coach), employer, business, or individual who will subsidize your idea for his or her own purposes.

Equity Financing and Debt Financing

There are two basic structures for obtaining cash to finance the launch of your business: equity financing and debt financing.

In equity financing, private investors such as family, friends, professional investors, or even employees buy a percentage of ownership of your business. Through equity financing, your business secures funding without incurring debt. Assets do not have to be used as a guarantee to obtain financing, and most often, investors do not have to be paid back if your company goes bankrupt. On the other hand, investors now own part of your business and may want to exert some form of control over it. You might have to accept direction from your investors and go along with decisions you might not agree with. You will have to give your investors their percentage of any profits from the business.

In debt financing, funds are borrowed and then repaid with interest over a designated period. Debt financing can be short term and require repayment in less than a year or long term and provide for repayment over a period of a year or more. The advantage of debt financing is that the lending institution does not receive any ownership stake in your business. This type of loan can be used to buy business assets, and interest paid on the loan is usually tax deductible. A disadvantage is that the bank might require the loan to be secured with an asset equal in value to the loan amount; some banks might require some form of personal guarantee. The business is obligated to make monthly payments on the debt, even when it is losing money. The interest you pay adds to the initial cost of starting your business.

Personal Investments and Loans

Nearly 80 percent of entrepreneurs rely on personal savings to begin a new enterprise. Using personal savings to start your business gives you complete control and ownership. You do not incur debt, and you do not share future profits with investors. If your business fails, you will have lost your savings, but you will not owe money to someone else.

You may already own a computer, a car, or real estate property that you can contribute to your business. Converting personal assets to business use is the same as giving your business cash. Not only will you avoid having to purchase these items, but also you will be able to depreciate them on your income tax returns. Your accountant can establish the conversion and depreciation schedules for you.

Consult an accountant about your plans. If you lend money to your company, you may be entitled to interest on the loan, along with repayment.

Home Equity Loans

You may be able to obtain a personal loan or a revolving line of credit from a bank using your home or another item of personal property as collateral. If you are unable to repay the loan, you risk losing the property. To estimate how much equity you have in your home, ask a real estate agent to look up the prices of similar homes that have sold in your area recently and subtract the amount you still owe on your mortgage. When you take out a home equity loan, the bank will probably have your home professionally appraised, and the appraised value may be less than the current market value. Look for a bank that does not charge closing costs or other fees for home equity loans. A revolving line of credit (RELOC) is a home equity loan that works something like a credit card. It allows you to borrow only what you need, for example, to buy computers or furniture, repay it at any time, and borrow again. You will have to make a minimum monthly payment. Any additional payments should be applied to the principal to reduce the amount of interest you pay and regain the equity on your home.

When you own your home outright, you can safely borrow a small percentage of the value because if something should go wrong in the future, you can refinance (repay the loan by taking out a new loan based on your remaining equity). If you own 20 percent or less of the equity in your home, never borrow against it. You will be able to borrow only a minimal amount and risk foreclosure if you are unable to repay the loan.

A benefit of a home equity loan is that the interest paid on it can be deducted from your taxable income as mortgage interest.

Business Credit Cards

When you register a new business, credit card companies often will send you offers for business credit cards. If you have good personal credit and a high enough credit limit, you may be able to borrow enough money to set up your office and begin your business using a business credit card. Be wary of high and fluctuating interest rates, and make sure you will be able to make the monthly payments until your business makes enough income to pay off the entire debt.

Remember that everything you buy using a credit card will cost you more because you will be paying high interest rates on your purchases.

Commercial Business Loans

If you have a good credit record, strong credentials, and a solid business plan, you can approach a bank about applying for a business loan. Commercial banks are looking for promising investments with minimal risk. A loan officer who recognizes that you have a good business idea and the knowledge and skills to make it succeed might be willing to work with you.

Start by showing your business plan to a loan officer from a bank and ask what you would have to do to qualify for a business loan. If your business plan looks promising, he or she will be happy to guide you through the application process and tell you what kind of documentation is required. You may have to approach several banks before you find one willing to give you a loan.

Your business plan should specify how much money you want to borrow and how you plan to use it. Do not ask for more than you need, but make sure you borrow enough to get your business up and running. If you borrow too little, you will have difficulty achieving your goals and paying back the loan.

Market conditions affect loan approval and denial rates, as well as how much money the bank is willing to lend (lower amounts in tough economic conditions and higher amounts when the economy is thriving). Banks look at the following factors when evaluating a loan application:

- **Credit history:** Banks gauge your ability to repay a loan by your credit history. If you have a history of paying back your debts, they will look more favorably on giving you a loan.

- **Collateral:** A bank may ask for collateral such as real estate or something else of value to secure the loan. If you are unable to repay the loan, the bank will recover its money by claiming the property and selling it.

- **Cosigning:** A bank might require that someone credit-worthy back you up by cosigning the loan. The cosigner becomes responsible for repaying the loan if you default.

- **History:** If you have a history of doing business with a bank, or of owning and operating a successful business, the bank it may be more willing to loan you money.

An institutional lender can become a strong ally if you use it exclusively for all of your banking and financial services. When you have paid off your first loan or are ready to refinance in order to expand your business, the bank will be ready to work with you. As you build a strong relationship with bank representatives, they may even refer clients to you. Try to get to know your bank manager on a personal level, and occasionally invite him or her out to lunch or for coffee. People do business with people they know and like. A bank manager who knows you well will be willing to go out of his or her way to help you. Bankers recognize the signs of careful preparation and planning. If you start building a relationship a few months before needing a loan and let your bank representative know you may be in the market for a loan once your plans are solidified, it may improve your chances of acceptance. The banker will know you have been working on your plans for some time and are not making a snap decision.

Both commercial banks and credit unions offer small business loans.

Before you seek financial assistance

The U.S. Small Business Administration suggests asking the following questions before seeking financial assistance:

- Do you need more capital, or can you manage existing cash flow more effectively?

- How do you define your need? Do you need money to expand or as a cushion against risk?

- How urgent is your need? You can obtain the best terms when you anticipate your needs rather than looking for money under pressure.

- How great are your risks? All businesses carry risks, and the degree of risk will affect cost and available financing alternatives.

- In what state of development is the business? Needs are most critical during transitional stages.

- For what purposes will the capital be used? Any lender will require that capital be requested for specific needs.

- What is the state of the financial planning industry? Depressed, stable, or growth conditions require different approaches to money needs and sources. Businesses that prosper while others are in decline will often receive better funding terms.

- How strong is your management team? Management is the most important element assessed by money sources.

- How does your need for financing mesh with your business plan?

Commercial banks

Commercial banks offer a variety of services, including business checking accounts, certificates of deposit (CDs), loans, and fiduciary services (the bank acts as trustee for another's assets). Banks accept bank drafts, issue business letters of credit, and offer credit cards and mortgages. The Federal Deposit Insurance Corporation (FDIC) insures commercial banks. You may already have a business relationship with a commercial bank if you are selling financial products.

Credit unions

A credit union is a cooperative whose members have partial ownership of the "bank." Earnings are divided among members in the form of dividends or reduced interest rates. Although there are always exceptions, it is common for a credit union to offer higher deposit rates and lower transaction fees than commercial banks. Credit unions tend to offer attractive deals for their members. Each credit union has its own requirements for becoming a member and being able to open an account and obtain a loan. For example, a teacher's credit union may require that you are a teacher in good standing in the county where the credit union is located. For some regional credit unions, you are eligible to join if you can show your address falls within the county served by the credit union. A credit union can accept more modest returns on its loans because it functions as a nonprofit organization with lower operating costs than commercial banks.

Not all credit unions are the same. Most are not insured through the FDIC. However, the National Credit Union Share Insurance Fund (NCUSIF) insures all federal credit unions and many of the state-chartered credit unions. The National Credit Union Administration (NCUA), the federal agency responsible for chartering and supervising all of the federal credit unions, administers NCUSIF. Most credit unions offer the same services as banks, including checking and credit cards, but use different terminology. Where a commercial bank refers to a "checking account," a credit union will call it a "share draft account." Credit unions are not as likely as banks to offer benefits such as more convenient banking hours for business owners. Compare the rates and fees of credit unions in your area with those of the larger commercial banks.

Government Sponsored Financing: SBA Loans

The U.S. Small Business Administration (SBA) provides assistance to small businesses and helps to educate small business owners. Unlike loans from traditional financial institutions, which often are short term with temporary lines of credit, the SBA offers long-term loan guarantee programs. The SBA is not the source of your loan but instead, coordinates a loan from a participating bank or institution. When an institution determines that a business is too much of a risk, the SBA will step in and make as much as a 90-percent guarantee to the bank that the SBA will pay off the loan if the business is unable to do so. The entrepreneur must prove through an extensive application process that he or she will be able to pay off the loan and have collateral to back it up.

SBA programs do not require a large down payment, whereas 20 to 30 percent is common for the conventional lending institutions. The typical down payment for an SBA loan is 10 percent, and an amortized term of up to 25 years may be offered. The SBA does not carry balloon loans that must be paid off in full after five or ten years when the loan reaches maturity. The SBA helps keep money accessible to and flowing through small businesses rather than encouraging businesses to deplete all of their capital making loan payments, which could stifle growth. These loans are compatible for small businesses as well as moderately small corporations. The SBA guarantees loans up to $5 million.

Talk to your bank about applying for a loan through the SBA. You must supply your bank lender with all the paperwork for the loan application, including your business plan and financial statements. If the bank is unable to extend you a loan, ask officers to consider your loan under the SBA's guaranty program. The SBA has several small business loan programs:

Basic 7(a) loan guaranty

This is SBA's primary business loan program. Although its maximum allowable loan is $2 million, it is the SBA's most flexible business loan program in its terms and eligibility requirements and is designed to accommodate a wide variety of financing needs. Most of these loans are given to serve functions such as working capital, machinery, equipment, furniture, renovation, new construction, and debt refinancing. Commercial lenders are the ones who actually make the loans and the determination for whom they will make loans to, but the government offers a guarantee for a percentage of the loan should the borrower default. For this particular loan program, the government can guarantee up to 75 percent of the total loan made to the business if it exceeds $150,000 and 85 percent for loans less than $150,000.

The most attractive features of the 7(a) is its low down payment, low interest rates compared to most banks, and an extended loan maturity (as many as ten years for working capital and 25 years for fixed assets). Should a business want to start an early payoff, a small percentage of the prepayment amount will be charged as a prepayment fee. The early payoff can come in handy when a business is experiencing fast growth and needs to refinance in order to support its expansion, and the small fee required to do this may be more than worthwhile.

Microloan program

This short-term loan offers small loans (up to $50,000) to small businesses that are starting up or growing, but the average microloan is about $13,000. Funds are made available to intermediary lenders that are nonprofit and community-based, and these lenders typically require some form of collateral. The loan can be used as working capital to fund the operations and to purchase inventory, supplies, equipment, furniture, or fixtures for the business. There are intermediaries for this type of loan available in most states, the District of Columbia, and Puerto Rico. The states where there is no intermediary include Alaska, Rhode Island, Utah, and West Virginia; Rhode Island and a section of West Virginia are currently accessing intermediaries in neighboring states.

Prequalification pilot loan program

This program allows a small business to have their loan applications analyzed and receive a potential blessing from the SBA before a lender or institution considers them. It covers loan applications in which the business owner is looking for funds of up to $250,000. Deciding factors may involve the applicant's credit, experience, reliability, and character.

This program can help an applicant who has relatively good credit and a semi-established business looking for expansion. The SBA will ask to see past financial records, ratios, history, and personal credit. The SBA will help determine which sections of the loan request are potential red flags for the bank and then recommend the most favorable terms the applicant should expect.

8(a) program

This program was specifically designed to help socially or economically disadvantaged people (minority entrepreneurs, business leaders, or persons with disabilities). These loans traditionally are used for a startup or expansion development. To qualify, a socially or economically disadvantaged person — not just a figurehead in the position — must own and control at least 51 percent of the business. Along these lines are additional assistance programs targeted to veterans, women, and handicapped persons.

Low-Doc program

The Low-Doc (short for low-document) program is set up to make the application process much simpler and quicker than traditional methods. It does this by reducing the size of the application form to one page for loans under $50,000. For larger loans of $50,000 to $100,000, an applicant receives the same one-page application, along with a request for his or her past three years of income tax returns. This program is the most popular in the SBA's history.

CAPLines

A CAPLines loan is an asset-based line of credit that allows businesses to manage short-term needs, such as continuing payroll and purchasing equipment. Typically, a business that is unable to qualify for other lines of credit, such as a builder or small company, might use this type of loan. The payback terms of a CAPLines loan are adjusted to fit seasonality and cash flow.

Other Forms of Loans and Grants

Not all loans come from the government or from a bank. You can go about obtaining the necessary money for your new business in several other ways.

Borrowing from family and friends

Many entrepreneurs get low-interest or interest-free loans from family members or friends to start a business. A family member or friend already knows you well and may have an interest in seeing you succeed.

Consider the possible consequences carefully before accepting a loan from friends or family members. Borrowing from people close to you can negatively affect your relationship if the lender is critical of you or scrutinizes you too closely. When you borrow from your family or friends, make it a legal transaction by putting all the terms in a written contract. Be sure to repay the loans as agreed.

Before accepting a loan from someone close to you, ask yourself:

- Will this person panic about money after investing?
- Does he or she understand the risks and benefits?

- Will he or she want to take control or become a nuisance?

- Would a failure ruin your relationship?

- Does this person bring something to the table, besides cash, that can benefit your company and you?

Private investors

Private investors are individuals or companies who lend money directly to a business in exchange for a share of the revenue or a high interest rate. Venture capitalists specialize in funding startups. They, typically, have a good working knowledge of the industry they are investing in and look for business opportunities that they believe have a good chance of succeeding. They usually insist on having a certain amount of control, and they sometimes want to be actively involved in the business or to mentor you. Negotiating a deal with a venture capitalist may mean giving up some of your freedom and having to defer to your investor when making business decisions. You can look for investors through websites, such as Fundingpost™ (**www.fundingpost.com**), 3iC LLC (**www.help-finance.com/who1.htm**), and at venture capital expos.

Angel investors are wealthy individuals who are willing to invest money in a project with the expectation of sharing in the business's future success. Angel investors are less likely than venture capitalists to interfere directly in the day-to-day affairs of the business and are willing to wait longer to see a return on their investments. Nevertheless, they can place demands and restrictions on you. Angel investors often are found by networking and word-of-mouth. Tell everyone, everywhere you go, that you are looking for funding to start a new business. An angel investor might be a friend or family member who wants to support your project or a professional contact that believes your business can be successful.

Whether you are borrowing money from a friend or a business consortium, get everything in writing, and have your lawyer look over the contract before you sign. Have a clear understanding of what is expected from each party, when the loan is to be repaid, and the amount of control the lender will have over your business affairs.

Grants and economic development programs

There are private organizations and public agencies that help businesses in exchange for "giving back" to the community. These organizations offer help in the form of:

- Direct grants that require no financial repayment

- Grants repaid from future revenues with no repayment requirement should your business fail

- Economic development programs designed to maximize your business's financial impact on the community

- Location grants that offer a financial incentive to locate your business in a specific area to provide economic stimulus to a community or city

- "Soft" loans with less stringent qualifications and "softer" terms and conditions, such as no-interest or low-interest loans

- Tax cuts, deferrals, and deductions that lower your business, personal, or property taxes

- Support in the form of free advice and access to resources that saves you consulting fees and improve your chances for business success

You might qualify to receive this kind of support by locating your office in an economically depressed area; offering low-cost or free services for special needs, low-income, or elderly clients; volunteering within your community; or mentoring others. Being a good citizen and showing your commitment to the community can enhance the reputation of your business and help to attract customers.

Other Ways to Save Money

If you do not want to deal with the hassle and repayments of getting a loan, you can find other ways to make sure you have the startup capital you need to ensure your business' success. Here are some ways you can economize and get ready to go into business for yourself.

Sharing ownership

Do you have a professional contact or a colleague who might be interested in going into business with you on a part-time or full-time basis? Perhaps you can join someone who already has an established financial service, such as an insurance agent or a debt counselor and offer your financial planning services as an extension of his or her business. Someone who is already operating a successful business might be willing to help finance your startup as a silent partner. They may even be able to provide you with office space and shared support staff.

Work for Someone Else

If you are anxious to work full-time as a financial planner but do not have the financial resources to strike out on your own, look for a large financial services firm or an established financial planning company that would be willing to take you on as an employee and pay you a salary or commissions. Working in someone else's business will help you hone your interpersonal skills and define your niche. While you are working and gaining experience, you can save up to start your own business or continue to seek financing for your own company. In the meantime, you will gain valuable experience and be coached by professionals who know the business well. Another advantage is that you do not have to have your own licenses to sell securities or insurance if you act as an agent for a licensed securities or insurance brokerage.

Start small and economize

Start your financial planning business by freelancing or working part-time while you support yourself with another job. Offer your services to friends and relatives and find new clients by networking — one job will lead to another. Rent a small office in a business center that provides a central reception area, secretarial, and telephone-answering services. Use a virtual telephone answering service to take calls from prospective clients and set up appointments. You can find business centers and virtual office services in business yellow pages or by searching on the Internet. As your client list grows and your income increases, you will arrive at a point where you have enough business to keep you working full-time.

Save money in every way you can. Take advantage of introductory offers, banking discounts and rebates (always read the fine print and mark any deadlines on your calendar). Convert furniture, computers, and other supplies you already own to business use instead of buying new ones. Look for discounted furniture at an office supply or warehouse furniture store or outlets that sell second-hand furniture and office equipment. Browse the classified ads on Craigslist. A business that is closing may be willing to accept a low price for its office furnishings. Barter your services for products and services your company needs. Join wholesale clubs, store discount programs, or professional associations that offer discounted prices or rewards for purchases. You may be able to rent equipment and computers or pay with an installment plan over several years.

Writing a Loan Proposal

Most investors or lending institutions require a business owner to write and submit a loan proposal when applying for financing. Although a family member or friend may not require a formal written loan proposal, it is best practice to write and submit one to anyone and everyone you do business with. The loan proposal allows you the opportunity to demonstrate why your business is a risk worth taking.

A loan proposal is a condensed version of your business plan. Try to be conservative in developing revenue estimates. When calculating your expenses, include accurate estimates of all possible costs. Avoid underestimating because that can cause you to run short of funds earlier than anticipated. The proposal should include a detailed explanation of how you came up with the figures.

Sample loan proposal

To give you an idea of what a loan proposal contains and its format, here is a sample. *(Please see the Sample Loan Proposal on the accompanying CD.)*

General information

- Name of business
- Name of owners/principals (whichever is applicable)
- Owner's Social Security number or EIN (whichever is applicable)
- Business address

Loan information

- Clearly state the purpose of your loan.
- State exact amount of funds requested.
- State the requested terms of the loan (i.e. length of loan and interest rate).
- List the collateral you will use to secure the loan (include current market values).
- State how much equity you will be contributing to this undertaking.

Business description

- Provide the history and nature of the business.
- State the legal structure of the business.
- Explain any future plans for the business and how the loan will benefit the business.

Market information

- Clearly define the services provided by your company.
- Discuss your business's market, stating your target customer base.
- Demonstrate the demand for your services.
- Identify your competitors, and explain how you are able to compete in the global marketplace.
- Identify your customers and how you are able to serve them.
- Discuss your marketing plan, and identify costs associated with it.

Business financial information

- Demonstrate ability to pay the loan through financial projections.
- For a startup loan:
  - Provide a projected balance sheet and income statement.
- For sole proprietors or partnerships:
  - Provide both your and the other owners' financial statements.
- For other loans:
  - Provide financial statements, income statements, and balance sheets for the past three years.
  - Provide tax returns for the past three years.

Other supporting documentation

- Provide copies of important legal documents, such as Articles of Incorporation and Fictitious Name registration.

Protecting Your Business: Insurance

Insurance protects your business from loss due to accidents, crime, lawsuits, and other unpredictable misfortunes. Insurance not only protects you, it ensures that money is available to pay medical and legal bills for injured parties and compensate investors or lenders for any losses they experience. For this reason, businesses are required by law to have certain types of insurance. Insurance laws vary by state. Many states have minimum business insurance standards, and some cities and localities impose more stringent requirements. Check with your personal insurance carrier first for business insurance information. If the carrier does not provide business insurance, ask for a referral from your personal insurance agent and fellow business owners.

At a minimum, a personal financial adviser should have comprehensive general liability insurance, vehicle insurance for travel to and from client meetings, and if the business is operated from a home-based office, home business insurance. Many insurance companies combine several types of insurance into a comprehensive Business Owners Policy (BOP) for which you pay a single premium.

Comprehensive general liability insurance

General liability insurance protects your business from liability for unexpected accidents and injuries caused by someone employed by your business or claims made by people who are injured or have accidents while on your business premises. It also protects you against losses due to crime or against legal action brought against you because of breaches of confidentiality or privacy. Review the policy carefully for exclusions that might leave you vulnerable. If your policy excludes damage caused by a drunken employee, for instance, you may not be covered if your associate has several drinks during lunch and then causes an accident. Compare quotes from two or three insurers before making a decision. If you are uncertain about how much liability coverage you need, consult your lawyer or another financial planner.

An insurance broker who specializes in small business coverage can help determine what you need. Ask questions, write down figures, and any coverage assurances given by the provider or broker, and then check those figures against the actual provisions in the policy.

The insurance company will probably require that all visitor areas should be clean and organized to prevent slips and falls. Bookshelves and heavy items such as televisions should be anchored to the wall or floor so they cannot tip over. Paper and electronic files should be secured and protected to prevent dishonest employees or hackers from gaining access to confidential information.

Professional liability insurance

Professional liability insurance protects a financial planner from legal action by clients who claim they received faulty or insufficient advice and from the consequences of negligence or theft by an employee. You may be required to be bonded if you are selling securities or other financial products. Employee Dishonesty Bonds reimburse employers for losses from employee fraud, theft, forgery, and embezzlement of company's cash and other assets.

Workers' compensation insurance

Workers' compensation insurance, or as it is commonly known, workers' comp, is required in every state. However, the structure of the insurance varies by state. Private insurance companies offer this coverage based on the number of employees on the payroll, the responsibilities of each individual, and the type of business. Some states require that coverage be obtained from the state government or one of its agencies. This insurance pays medical expenses and lost wages for workers hurt while performing job duties for your business. Workers' comp generally covers employees that are on company trips or events that fall outside of working hours, but not all policies extend coverage to offsite locations. There are exclusions for certain categories of workers — independent contractors and volunteers, for instance — but again, check your state's laws. Business owners are generally exempt from this type of coverage.

Home-based business insurance

Homeowner's policies rarely cover business losses. Check with your insurance agent to see if anything in your home office is covered by your homeowner's policy. The typical homeowner's policy excludes home-based business losses, including equipment, theft, loss of data, and personal injury. Unfortunately, many companies that provide homeowner's insurance do not offer business coverage, so you may have to work with an insurance carrier other than the one that handles your personal insurance needs.

Crime insurance

Crime insurance provides coverage if an employee commits a crime. In a financial planning business, the most common crimes arise from employee dishonesty and electronic theft by outsiders who hack into computers or use clients' personal information to steal money from their accounts. You can be held responsible for the actions of an employee if he or she should steal, vandalize customer property, or deliberately harm someone while with customers. General liability insurance may not cover theft or other criminal acts by employees.

You can prevent embezzlement by gathering detailed personal information from job applicants, conducting criminal background checks, checking references, and building a system of checks and balances into your accounting system. *See the checklists for accounting fraud on the Companion CD.* Electronic files on your computers should be protected with strong passwords, and access should only be given to trusted employees. Online banking systems and brokerage accounts typically, are protected with strong security, and these companies are responsible for losses that occur if their security is breached. However, a dishonest employee with access to passwords and customers' personal information could go into customers' accounts and divert funds into his or her own bank account.

TIP: Do not become a victim of fraud.

It is happening every day, in companies of all sizes: a trusted employee is discovered to have diverted tens or hundreds of thousands of dollars of the company's money into his or her own pocket. More than 96 percent of these employees have no criminal background; they just find themselves in a situation where it is easy to steal and cannot resist the temptation. Every year U.S. businesses lose an estimated 7 percent of their annual revenues to fraud.

Do not let someone steal your hard-earned money. Fraud occurs when the accounting system is poorly organized and when one individual is given control of multiple accounting functions, such as approving invoices and writing checks. The best way to prevent and detect fraud is to review your accounts regularly for irregularities and to require more than one person to approve expenditures. All expenses should be documented with sales receipts and/or invoices. Have an outside accountant review your account records from time to time, especially if one individual is doing all the bookkeeping. Follow your intuition; if you sense that something is wrong, investigate. An honest mistake can be discovered quickly, and the person's name cleared. A dishonest employee could continue to undermine your business for years and deprive you and your hard-working employees of their rightful earnings.

Key person insurance

Lenders who provide capital for businesses may require key person insurance. Key person insurance is a type of life insurance policy for the person whose absence from the company would cause it to fail. Most often, that person is you or your partner. If you have borrowed money to start or operate your business, the lender may require you to have life insurance as a guarantee of payment if anything were to happen to you. Coverage under these policies can range from $500,000 to $10 million. The rule of thumb is to match the policy coverage amount with the key person's salary (or income). Some business owners choose to carry coverage that is up to 15 times their salary for extended coverage. Generally, small businesses implement key person insurance policies for double or triple the salary of the owner. The average key person insurance policy costs less than $1,000 per year but can vary according to the amount of coverage; some cost up to 3 percent of the face value of the policy.

Business interruption insurance

Business interruption insurance assures you an income if your business is shut down by fire, natural disaster, or another catastrophe. If your equipment and vehicles already are covered, you may not want to duplicate coverage, so consult your insurance provider or broker for details. This type of insurance is a good idea if your business is located in an area prone to natural disasters, such as hurricanes, ice storms, tornadoes, or earthquakes.

Vehicle insurance

Generally, a personal financial planner and his or her employees insure their own vehicles with personal coverage because there is no need for a specialty vehicle to perform company duties. If you are a sole proprietor, let your current insurance carrier know you will be using the vehicle for business purposes, such as going back and forth to client meetings.

Any additional coverage will be added to your personal policy, and the premium may increase with the added coverage. The premium will reflect the number of miles you regularly drive for your business. Increasing personal vehicle coverage is typically less expensive than buying business vehicle insurance coverage.

Business vehicle insurance is the commercial version of the insurance you have on your private vehicle. The same considerations apply to your premiums: type of vehicle, history of claims, mileage, location, and drivers. If employees drive your company vehicles, their driving records, along with yours, will be taken into consideration when calculating your insurance rates. When numerous people drive company vehicles, this can increase the cost of vehicle coverage.

CASE STUDY: "FINANCIAL PEACE COACH" AIMS TO HELP OTHERS SIMPLIFY THEIR LIVES

BeckyJohnson, CFP, CSACEP, CDFA, financial advocate
Dave Ramsey, Certified Financial Counselor, Crossroads Financial Solutions, president
5350 Tomah Drive, Suite 3000
Colorado Springs, CO 80918
Phone 719-265-6363
Fax:719-265-9776
Becky@CoachBeckyJ.com
www.CoachBeckyJ.com

After Becky Johnson and her husband experienced personal tax problems, including garnishment, as young newlyweds in the late 1970s, the couple suddenly found themselves owing $5,000 for self-employment taxes. Johnson's husband suggested she read a big, fat tax book to complement the information she had acquired in high school business classes. As it turned out, Johnson enjoyed the big, fat tax book so much that she enrolled in tax and tax preparation classes. However, Johnson quickly found herself frustrated because she was approaching the preparation of tax returns based on the past rules and regulations rather than those currently in effect. This was a costly mistake. While keeping up with her tax studies and the ever-changing tax laws, Johnson steered her career toward financial planning.

When Johnson started out in the financial planning industry, she was trained to deal with overall financial planning issues. During her career, Johnson earned several certifications, as a financial planner, investment adviser, senior citizen advocate, and estate planner. All of these certifications allowed Johnson to specialize in specific areas when providing advice to clients.

After dealing with client issues that fell more on the asset side of the balance, Johnson became interested in dealing with the liabilities side of the balance sheet. Johnson enrolled in a workshop specifically targeted at getting rid of clients' debt. In 2006, Johnson gave up her investment license and turned to a specialization in helping clients manage their finances from a debt perspective rather than an investment-oriented approach. This move forced Johnson to change to a fee-based system.

Johnson also trained in mediation, which has helped her in her relations with clients. She sees many couples that have been having relationship problems because of money. To illustrate some of the things Johnson helps clients accomplish, one couple paid her to go through their divorce agreement and explain the tax ramifications involved in the custodial arrangements. Another family of two was spending $3,000 a month on groceries; when the woman came up with a number for the budget breakout, even she was shocked.

Johnson's income is earned by charging a fee for her time, and people really seem to appreciate that — especially those who are cost-conscious. Sometimes financial planners, even when they are fee-based, are trying to sell investments, insurance, or other catchall financial products such as living trusts, which have additional costs. Although there is supposed to be full disclosure, people sometimes get home and realize they signed off on something that costs them 5.75 percent of the initial transaction. After clients decide to work with Johnson, they enjoy six months of scheduled follow-up meetings to address their financial plan.

CHAPTER 6

Finding a Location and Setting Up Your Office

The physical location of your financial planning business will be important to your success. Although some of your services can be offered on the Internet or over the telephone, the individual attention given to each client is what distinguishes a personal financial planner from a stockbroker or a banker. You will be conducting personal interviews with each new client and meeting with existing clients at regular intervals and whenever their financial situations change. Your place of business must be physically accessible to your clients, and you need to be able to meet with them without having to travel long distances. For this reason, your office should be located in the same area where your target clientele live or work.

Your physical address also makes a statement to prospective clients about the nature of your business. If your business will be managing the wealth of affluent clients, you need a prestigious office in the business district or in an affluent neighborhood. If you are working with retirees, locate your business in an area where many retired people live, and where they can park conveniently and feel comfortable coming in to your office. If your specialty is young families or families with special-needs children, it is best to be in a central location where people from many neighborhoods can easily reach your office.

Before you begin shopping for real estate, establish a profile of your typical client and consider where people who fit your profile will be found. Make a written list of broad categories of potential clients. Then add details for each category using trade publications, phone books, the Internet, and your network of contacts. Writing everything down will help you form a clear picture of the size your potential market. Finally, research your competition. Find out what services other financial planners in the area offer for your potential clients. If several others offer the same services, identify the qualities that make your business unique and set you apart from the competition.

Find out what fees your competitors are charging. Use these fees in conjunction with your potential client list to calculate an income estimate for your business. Using conservative figures, estimate monthly, quarterly, and annual income. Make allowances for lower revenues during the months and years while your new business is becoming established. Compare your projected income with your income from your current job to see if your potential client base will be adequate to support a viable business. Doing work you love can be personally rewarding, but it is also important to determine that doing what you love will be profitable.

Are you planning to open your business in the town where you currently live, or are you willing to relocate in order to be near a certain type of client? If you intend to stay put, research the demographics of your area carefully and observe the locations of other businesses and the neighborhoods where your target clients live and work. What groups of businesses, organizations, or individuals need the financial services you are thinking of providing? Create your business to serve needs already existing in your community.

If you are willing to relocate, look for a city or town with a population that matches the profile of your target market. For example, communities of wealthy professionals exist in large cities, while retirees congregate in smaller towns in warm places such as Florida, Arizona, and California. Once you establish your business, you must remain in the same area for a number of years to build up a client base — moving again would mean leaving your clients behind and starting all over. It is important to study an area carefully before you commit yourself to setting up a business there.

Researching Business Location Information

The U.S. Census Bureau (**www.census.gov**) supplies information such as population, median age and income, and employment statistics. You can also use a free trial subscription with DemographicsNow (**www.demographicsnow.com**) to look for physical locations that match the demographics of your target market. For example, if you want to specialize in working with executive level women between the ages of 40 and 55, you will want to locate the geographical areas that have the highest concentrations of these types of women.

Another source of local demographic information is your Chamber of Commerce. To find a Chamber of Commerce in another area, use an online search such as the one on Business Finance.com (**www.businessfinance.com/chambers-of-commerce.htm**). Most Chambers of Commerce gather data related to the businesses in their membership area. If you intend to target business owners, you can see what kinds of businesses exist in your town. Business information can also help you to evaluate whether a particular area is a good target market for you and what kind of competition you might face. For example, the presence of financial planning businesses similar to yours indicates a potential market exists there. Study these businesses closely to see how successful they are and whether they have already saturated the market. If you intend to specialize in socially responsible investments and there is a large concentration of green living businesses in the area, you can conclude your target audience exists there.

The American Community Survey (**www.census.gov/acs**) provides additional information from the supplemental census survey, including demographics by county and metropolitan statistical areas (MSAs).

You can also search the membership directory and read helpful articles on the website of the national Financial Planning Association (**www.fpanet.org**). Based in Denver, Colorado, the leadership and advocacy organization for professional financial planning has nearly 100 local chapters representing more than 25,000 members. Organizations catering to financial planning professionals often conduct surveys and share information that includes client demographics, financial planning best practices, case studies, and market projections. Some organizations require you to become a member in order to access this information.

Some other places to look for useful information include:

- **CenStats Databases (http://censtats.census.gov)**: Economic and demographic information you can compare by county

- **County Business Patterns (www.census.gov/econ/cbp/index.html):**
Economic information reported by industry, including the number
of establishments, employment, and payroll for more than 40,000
ZIP codes across the country. Metro Business Patterns provides the
same data for MSAs.

- American FactFinder (**http://factfinder.census.gov**): A new
FactFinder that will allow you to search U.S. Census data by topic,
geography, population groups, and industry codes

Fortune's top ten cities for small businesses

In November 2009, *Fortune Small Business* published lists of the top U.S. cities for growing a small business. *FSB* named top ten big cities and 20 each of the best small and mid-sized cities based on numbers of small businesses and demographic information including income, population, and U.S. Census county business pattern figures. These lists show the local population and number of small businesses for each location.

FSB's ranking of the top ten big places in the United States in which to launch a small business is:

Rank	City	Population	No. of small businesses
1	Oklahoma City, OK	1,206,142	31,139
2	Pittsburgh, PA	2,351,192	57,272
3	Raleigh, NC	1,088,765	27,659
4	Houston, TX	5,728,143	112,748
5	Hartford, CT	1,190,512	28,609
6	Washington, DC	5,358,130	134,245
7	Charlotte, NC	1,701,799	42,926
8	Austin, TX	1,652,602	37,296
9	New York, NY	19,006,798	516,827
10	Baltimore, MD	2,667,117	64,481

Top 20 mid-sized places in which to launch a small business:

Rank	City	Population	No. of small businesses
1	Huntsville, AL	395,645	8,995
2	Lafayette, LA	259,073	8,113
3	Omaha, NE	837,925	20,990
4	Clarksville, TN	261,220	4,136
5	Peoria, IL	372,487	8,520
6	Lexington, KY	453,424	11,248
7	Killeen, TX	378,935	5,574
8	Des Moines, IA	556,230	14,174
9	Baton Rouge, LA	774,327	16,860
10	Lincoln, NE	295,486	7,821
11	Jackson, MS	537,285	12,409
12	Lubbock, TX	270,610	6,571
13	Fayetteville, AR	443,976	5,856
14	Wilmington, NC	347,012	10, 242
15	Durham, NC	489,762	11,007
16	McAllen, TX	726,604	10,028
17	El Paso, TX	742,062	12,488
18	Wichita, KS	603,716	14,091
19	Tulsa, OK	916,079	23,310
20	Madison, WI	561,505	14,654

Top twenty small places in which to launch a small business

North Dakota and South Dakota combined have five, and Iowa has three.

Rank	City	Population	No. of small businesses
1	Billings, MT	152,005	5,687
2	Bismarck, ND	104,944	3,231
3	Fargo, ND	195,685	5,803
4	Rapid City, SD	122,522	4,130
5	Sioux Falls, SD	232,930	6,580
6	Midland, TX	129,494	4,151
7	Morgantown, WV	118,506	2,616
8	Dubuque, IA	92,724	2,585
9	Hattiesburg, MS	140,781	3,274
10	Missoula, MT	107,320	4,183
11	Tuscaloosa, AL	206,765	4,272
12	Bowling Green, KY	117,947	2,704
13	Grand Forks, ND	92,279	2,460
14	Logan, UT	125,070	3,254
15	Abilene, TX	159,521	3,752
16	Auburn-Opelika, AL	133,010	2,321
17	Waterloo, IA	164,220	3,931
18	Ames, IA	86,754	1,911
19	Charlottesville, VA	194,391	5,643
20	Jefferson City, MO	146,363	3,572

Locations with highest per-capita income

Want to go where the money is? This is certainly a factor to consider in forming a personal financial planning business. According to *FSB's* 2009 research results, the following metro areas have residents with the highest annual incomes. (Although California tops the list with seven places, Colorado, Florida, and Texas each have two.)

Rank	Metro area	Per-capita income	Per-capita income growth (2002-2007)
1	Bridgeport, CT	$81,576	36%
2	Naples, FL	$63,276	50%
3	San Francisco, CA	$60,983	32%
4	Vero Beach, FL	$59,419	49%
5	San Jose, CA	$59,338	30%
6	Washington, DC	$54,971	29%
7	Boston, MA	$53,443	26%
8	Midland, TX	$52,974	63%
9	New York City, NY	$52,855	31%
10	Casper, WY	$52,543	55%
11	Trenton, NJ	$52,255	25%
12	Boulder, CO	$51,388	28%
13	Napa, CA	$51,218	35%
14	Seattle, WA	$49,401	29%
15	Santa Cruz, CA	$48,337	29%
16	Hartford, CT	$48,330	27%
17	Bradenton, FL	$48,255	29%

Rank	Metro area	Per-capita income	Per-capita income growth (2002-2007)
18	Barnstable Town, MA	$47,640	26%
19	Santa Barbara, CA	$47,302	46%
20	Minneapolis, MN	$46,752	23%
21	Denver, CO	$46,682	20%
22	Houston, TX	$46,471	35%
23	Santa Rosa, CA	$46,325	27%
24	Baltimore, MD	$45,887	28%
25	Oxnard, CA	$45,694	33%

For the 11th year, in 2009 *Forbes* magazine also weighed in with its own list of the ten best U.S. metro and small metro areas in which to start a business. Criteria for the ratings included local cost of doing business, crime rate, education attainment, living costs, projected income, and job growth. You might want to also add some local market research on per-capita income levels, housing prices, family sizes, and other factors likely to impact business. Two of the areas in the list were in South Dakota and two were in Indiana.

Named as Best Small Metro Cities to Work were:
1. Sioux Falls, SD
2. Greenville, NC
3. Morgantown, WV
4. Bloomington, IN
5. Columbia, MO
6. Bismarck, ND
7. Fargo, ND
8. Lafayette, IN
9. Iowa City, IA
10. Auburn, AL

Of the communities named as Best Metro Cities to Work, three were in North Carolina and two were in Colorado. The cities were:

- Raleigh, NC
- Fort Collins, CO
- Durham, NC
- Fayetteville, AR
- Lincoln, NE
- Asheville, NC
- Des Moines, IA
- Austin, TX
- Boise, ID
- Colorado Springs, CO

Researching a site for your office

Because financial planning typically involves face-to-face meetings with clients, most financial planners establish a professional office from which to run their business. Invest time and effort to find the best physical location for your office. A financial planning business does not rely on walk-in traffic as much as a retail store, nail salon, or florist does. However, your office is where the majority, if not all, of your client meetings will occur, so your location should be mutually convenient for you and your clients. Exposure on a busy road is somewhat beneficial because people driving or walking past your office will read your sign and become aware of your existence, but most of your clients will find you through a business directory or a recommendation from a friend.

Factors to consider in evaluating a potential business site include:

- Whether it is in a downtown, commercial, or historic district
- Near government offices, professional services, or nearby shopping centers
- What educational institutions and degree programs, health care, or military facilities are in the community

Your Temporary Office

Set up a temporary office in a room at home from which to conduct your preliminary research before forming your personal financial planning business. Set aside enough space for all of your basic equipment and enough room to spread out your research materials on a desk or table. If you are working with a partner or working with clients from a home-based office, you will need an area where private discussions can take place. Although you can meet with colleagues or clients at the local library or coffee shop, public venues do not ensure confidentiality and privacy.

Remember that in order to claim tax deductions for a home office, you must have a dedicated area in the home that is used for business, and the office equipment, computer, and telephone must be used primarily for the business.

Items you need for a home office include:

- A desk or table with a comfortable chair
- A filing cabinet (or some strong paper ream boxes)
- A printer/copier/scanner combination with fax capability, if possible, or a telephone with fax and answering machine capability
- A desktop computer or a laptop
- Internet access
- Telephone, either land line or cell (a headset can be useful)

Look for a good computer service person that can help install business software systems and show you how to use them. Advertise in classified ads such as Craigslist (**www.craigslist.org**), look for listings in local newspapers, or ask other professionals for recommendations. Computer stores often sell subscriptions to technical services that install software and provide technical support by phone.

Internet access is vital for a financial planning business. If you are in a rural area where high-speed Internet is not available through your telephone service provider or cable network, invest in a USB broadband connection device and cellular phone service. You can get Internet access through a satellite receiver, but you may pay a setup cost in addition to monthly fees.

If you are going to set up your office at home initially, it is a good idea to install a separate business telephone line. Having your business voice mail pick up when you are not available is more professional than a family member answering the phone and taking a message for you. First impressions count, and a voice-mail service can give your callers the impression they are contacting a professional office.

If you are doing work from home for any financial services company, you can probably claim a tax deduction for the cost of your office furnishings and equipment. Read *IRS Publication 587, Business Use of Your Home* (**www.irs.gov/pub/irs-pdf/p587.pdf**) before you set up your office.

Home Office

More than half of America's small businesses are home-based, according to the Small Business Administration. A home office is a feasible alternative for a personal financial planner practicing alone, providing you can invite clients to visit you in an attractive, businesslike space and that your community allows home-based businesses. Many communities place restrictions on businesses based in private homes, mostly because of traffic, parking, and other issues associated with operating a busy practice in a residential neighborhood. Check with local and zoning officials.

The advantages of a home office are that you do not have to pay an additional rent (or mortgage payment), you do not have to commute, and you qualify for some tax benefits. Remember, however, that your office is the setting in which you form a professional relationship with your clients. The appearance of your home and your office convey something about what the client can expect from that relationship. Ringing doorbells and the presence of children or pets can be suggestive of competing needs and agendas. Conducting a client through your living room to a spare bedroom converted into an office may not be the best preamble for a conversation about the client's financial assets. If the atmosphere of your home and office does not match the image you are trying to portray, it may be difficult for you to gain your clients' confidence.

Home office checklist

- ❏ Do you have an enclosed or private area (preferably with a door) where you can shut out the outside world when it is time to work?

- ❏ Does the home office provide enough space for a desk, computer, printer, and phone?

- ❏ Do you have the ability to add another phone line to the office?

- ❏ Is the space heated and air-conditioned?

- ❏ Do you have storage space for files and supplies?

Flextime Office Space

In most cities, you can rent flextime office space or share office space with other businesses. Look for these facilities under "Office Rentals" in the yellow pages of your local phone book or on the Internet. Some flextime offices have "flex" in the name, but others use the term "executive," "executive suite," "ready-to-go," or "virtual office." Shared space options allow you to rent a cubicle or room in an office building for a monthly fee. In addition to dedicated workspaces, these facilities also have receptionists and telephone answering services to answer your business calls and forward them to you wherever you are or to take a message if you are unavailable. Generally, shared space options also provide limited administrative support to help you with tasks such as making copies, sending faxes, and creating correspondence. The flex space also provides you with a business mailing address where clients can send mail and packages, and someone is at the location to sign for and accept these deliveries.

A flextime office space provides your business with a professional façade. A receptionist answers your phone. You have a professional environment in which to conduct meetings and a place to do your work. Furniture, telephone lines, and Internet service already are installed. Some flextime offices allow renters to obtain space on an as-needed basis. Rather than pay a monthly fee for a dedicated space, you may have the option to use the facilities when and if you need them. You can use the mail and receptionist services and book office space or a conference room only when you need them.

Flextime office space checklist

- ❏ What space is available to you?

- ❏ What office equipment is included?

- ❏ Do you have to pay a monthly fee, or can you on an as-needed basis?

- ❏ Is there a dedicated line for your business? If yes, does your payment include someone to answer the line, take messages, and transfer the calls to you?

- ❏ Is there storage space for files and supplies?

Shared Office Space

Consider sharing office space with another professional such as an accountant or attorney. Many professional service firms rent and occupy office space too large for their immediate needs, which leaves unused office space. These professionals often are willing to rent out the extra space, which can mean you obtain an office inside a professional building at a reduced rate. Depending on your arrangement with the professional you are renting the space from, you may be able to share a receptionist and administrative support services.

Shared office space checklist

- ❏ What space is available to you?

- ❏ What office equipment is included (desk, computer, printer, and phone)?

- ❏ What is the monthly payment?

❑ Is there a dedicated phone number for your business? If yes, does your rent include someone to answer the line, take messages, and transfer the calls to you?

❑ Can you place a business sign outside the office door or on the building?

Formal and Professional Office

Rent, lease, or buy an office space in an existing building or a stand-alone building. A formal office can be a condo, office space, entire floor of an office building, or a storefront in a retail complex occupied by stores and other professionals such as real estate and insurance agents. You could gain more exposure for your business by opening an office near another financial service professional, such as an accountant, estate attorney, or insurance agent. Because you all have the same target market, you have a good chance of landing business when clients come to meet with one of the other professionals in the same office complex or retail center. Because most office spaces are completely unfurnished and without any type of support staff, you will have to furnish the office yourself and hire the staff you need. The primary disadvantage to having a formal office is all of the costs involved in establishing and maintaining it.

Costs

Some of the costs of a formal office space include:

- Upfront costs and down payment for a mortgage, lease, or rental payment (a percentage of the purchase price or first, last, and current month's rent payment)

- Insurance costs for keeping the office (liability, fire, theft)

- Installation of phone lines

- Purchase of furniture, equipment, and office decorations

- Alarm system and locks

- Employment of administrative staff

- Housekeeping/cleaning services

- Amenities such as a fridge, coffee maker, and microwave

Formal office space checklist

❏ What else does the rental space include (water, utilities)?

❏ What is the monthly payment?

❏ On top of the rental payment, what is it going to cost for electricity, phone service, cleaning, staffing, and other expenses?

❏ Will I need to hire staff to help run the office? If yes, how much will this cost for salary and benefits?

❏ Can you place a business sign outside the office door or on the building?

❏ Is the office a short commute from my home?

❏ Is the office conveniently located for business meetings with clients and vendors?

❏ Is the office located near related businesses that may be a referral source for business?

Compare and Contrast

In order to choose the best space for your new business, here are some charts that compare the advantages and disadvantages of each type of office:

HOME OFFICE	
PROS	**CONS**
✓ Saves you from having to pay rent for an office	✓ Blurs the line between your personal and business life
✓ Besides being convenient, saves time and money because you do not have to commute	✓ Is not particularly impressive to clients
✓ You can claim a federal tax deduction when you have dedicated space for your office in your home.	✓ Requires installation of additional phone lines and uses space in the home for business purpose

FLEXTIME OFFICE SUITES

PROS	CONS
✓ Provides a professional front	✓ Costs can range from a couple hundred to $1,000 a month
✓ Includes office furniture and supplies	✓ May be limitations on the personal items you can leave behind because the space is shared with others
✓ Some administrative support	
✓ Offers a dedicated work space in a professional environment	
✓ Reduces the cost of having to rent an entire office on your own	✓ Has office hours, so if you are inspired to work at midnight, you probably are not going to be able to access the building.
✓ Reduces the cost of having to hire staff such as a receptionist or administrative support	✓ Have to commute to work
	✓ Must share items such as the fax machine
✓ Allows you to separate your business and personal life	✓ Have to pay rent

SHARED OFFICE

PROS	CONS
✓ Provides a professional environment at a lower rate than renting your own office	✓ Have to commute to work
	✓ Must share items such as the fax machine
✓ Allows you to separate your business and personal life	✓ Clients might notice the sign on the office has the name of the firm you are renting from rather than your business name.
✓ Depending on the type of firm you rent from, may be a referral source of business for you	
	✓ Have to pay rent

FORMAL OFFICE	
PROS	**CONS**
✓ Provides a professional work environment	✓ More expensive than any other office option available
✓ Gives your business further exposure	✓ Distractions such as package deliveries, the cleaning crew, and your administrative staff
✓ Allows you to separate your business and personal life	✓ Have to pay rent or a mortgage
	✓ No support staff
	✓ Have to commute to work

Furniture, Equipment, and Software

Whether you establish your personal financial planning business in a home office or rent an office space, these are the minimal necessities to get started:

❑ Phone

❑ Fax machine, printer, scanner, or all-in-one machine

❑ Computer (PC or laptop) with Internet access

❑ Calculator (10-key)

❑ Personal digital assistant (PDA) or organizer

❑ Desk

❑ Chair

❑ Bookshelf

❑ Filing system

- ❑ Pens
- ❑ Paper
- ❑ Envelopes
- ❑ File folders

Useful software

Financial planners use a variety of software programs, many of which integrate with online banking and other sources of information. Some software can be purchased in a box or as a download for a fixed price; other programs are customized to fit each user's requirements. Some software programs store all data on your computers; other software companies store data in the "cloud" on their own servers where you can access it from any electronic device at any time. Prices vary according to the complex the softw te and the amount of d ta you are managing. f you have working a finance professional, ou probably already wn some o software nd know how to use it You will need softwa : to do fina analyses, le and organize docume ts, keep track of your ients, and reports and presentations.

Customer relations management (CRM)

CRM software uses a database of linked tables to organize client information, keep in contact with clients, and produce reports for them. You can send out automated e-mail and statements, maintain notes about each client, pull up reports with a click of your mouse, and keep a calendar of scheduled meetings and reviews. These are the CRM software programs most popular with financial planners:

ACT!	www.act.com
ACT4Advisors	www.act4advisors.com
Junxure	www.junxure.com
Redtail CRM	www.redtailtechnology.com
Web IS Pocket Informant	www.pocketinformant.com

Document management software

Financial planners deal with many types of documents, including scanned images, business cards, Word, Excel, PDF, CAD, e-mail, photos, and faxes. Document management software helps to store and organize these documents so the information in them can easily be searched and retrieved.

Cabinet NG CNG®-SAFE	www.cabinetng.com/products/cng_safe.php
Financeware® Finance File Manager	www.financefilemanager.com
SunGard LockBox	www.sungard.com
Worldox® software	www.worldox.com

Financial analysis software

Financial analysis software uses financial data to analyze investment portfolios, make projections, and recommend asset allocations to achieve financial goals.

Finance Logix® Retirement Planner	www.financelogix.com
Morningstar® Portfolio Strategist	http://corporate.morningstar.com/ib/asp/ subject.aspx?xmlfile=1387.xml
SunGard PlanningStation	www.sungard.com
WealthTec Foundations	www.wealthtec.com/foundations.htm

Financial Planning Presentation Software

An important aspect of personal financial planning is presenting your reports and evaluations to your clients in an impressive format that can be clearly understood. Presentation software is used to create slide shows, charts, and visual presentations.

Financial planning presentation software	Component in financial planning software programs
Microsoft PowerPoint	**http://office.microsoft.com/en-us/ powerpoint**
MoneyTree™ Silver Financial Planner	**www.moneytree.com**

Word Processing Software

Financial planners need powerful word processing program that make it easy to write, edit, and print reports, charts, letters, contract, and other important documents. Financial analysis software program have report features that can be used for this purpose, and some contain templates for contracts and legal documents. The most commonly used word processing program is Microsoft Word.

Automatic Data Processing ProxyEdge	**www.broadridge-ir.com**
Microsoft Word	**http://office.microsoft.com/en-gb/word**

Accounting Software Programs

Accounting software packages offer complete accounting systems that do just about everything: keep track of income, expenses, and sales tax; create invoices; do your payroll; process credit card transactions; import data from your bank statements and online shopping carts; print checks; produce instant customized reports; and create budgets, forecasts, and business plans.

One of the most widely used packages, known for its versatility and ease of use, is QuickBooks™ financial software. The basic version of this program, QuickBooks Pro, sells for less than $230 at office supply retailers. An online version is available starting at $10 per month. QuickBooks' Premier Edition is a complete accounting system that sells for approximately $400. QuickBooks also can be purchased online directly from the QuickBooks website at **www.quickbooks.intuit.com**, or other sites such as Amazon.com (**www.amazon.com**).

Another popular accounting package is Sage Peachtree Complete Accounting 2011 (**www.peachtree.com**), which sells for about $300 and offers more inventory options than Quickbooks. Although the setup is a little complicated, it is easy to use once you have it up and running.

You can find in-depth reviews of the top ten small business accounting software packages at Top Ten Reviews™ (**http://accounting-software-review.toptenreviews.com**).

All of these software packages have live support options and add-ons such as credit card processing services for an additional cost. They can be customized to fit your business needs. Have an accountant or someone who knows the program well help you set it up so it does exactly what you need it to do. Once the program is set up, all you have to do is enter your records on a regular basis.

Setting the scene: decorating your office to appeal to your clients

Most clients form their first impression of your business from what they see when they walk into your office. How you decorate your office can influence a client's decision to use (or not to use) your services. Although you want to convey the impression that your business is successful, overly extravagant furnishings suggest you are earning too much money by overcharging your clients or that you are financially irresponsible. Your office should have a pleasant and professional atmosphere without being intimidating. Financial planners agree that investing a few thousand dollars to furnish your office tastefully pays off in the end. You will be spending many hours there, and your clients will be coming there to discuss confidential matters that are important to them, so the office should reflect something of both your personality and theirs.

Here are some tips for decorating and arranging your office:

- **Keep your office clean and neat.** Always keep your office looking neat and organized. All visible areas, such as carpets, tabletops, and windowsills should be clean. Do not leave stacks of files and papers on your desk in the room where you meet with clients. They will feel you are overworked and will not devote enough time to their affairs or that you are disorganized and could misplace important papers. A career in finance requires self-discipline and careful attention to detail; your office should reflect that.

- **Avoid making a strong personal statement.** You might be proud of the moose head over your mantelpiece, but it could be a real turn-off for a potential client who hates hunting. Be careful about advertising your hobbies or political beliefs. Your clients might not share your love for motorcycles or appreciate your souvenirs from the Democratic National Convention. A client could feel antagonized by your football memorabilia if his grandson plays for a rival team. It is all right to reveal something about your personal interests, but remember that though some clients might be enthusiastic, you could alienate others who do not share your views.

- **One family photo is enough.** Too many photos of your spouse and children placed around your office are distracting and give the impression that you are so caught up in your family relationships you will not focus enough attention on the client.

- **Do not show off too much.** Although a framed diploma or certification hung on a wall shows you are well qualified for your job, a wall full of awards and certificates implies you are self-centered and full of your own accomplishments. Nobody likes that.

- **Choose colors and furnishings wisely.** Keep the furnishings simple and dignified, and choose neutral colors for the walls. Remember that light colors make a room look larger and brighter. Avoid artwork that might be offensive to some people, such as paintings of nudes.

The goal in decorating your office is to make clients feel welcome and at ease and to focus all attention on their concerns. A clean, peaceful, and well-organized office will make clients more receptive to what you have to say and more likely to trust you.

CHAPTER 7

Pricing, Payment, and Managing Costs

Learning how to price your services is crucial to your success as a personal financial planner. If you have always worked for someone else, you may not know how to calculate your fees so you can bring in enough income to support yourself, your family, and your business. In addition to helping your clients manage their finances, you now have several other jobs: drawing up contracts, monitoring your business expenses, collecting payments, paying taxes, and paying bills and employee salaries.

You must price your services so you are earning enough to cover your monthly operating expenses and pay your salary while remaining competitive with other financial planners in your area. It is important to be realistic about what your clients are willing and able to pay. If your prices are higher than those of other planners, the quality and depth of your services should be greater to justify the extra expense.

If you are not already working as a financial planner in your area and your specialty, do careful research to determine how much you can expect to charge your clients before you commit to an expensive office property or hire an employee. It is better to start simply and expand your business when you know how much you can expect to earn and what your real operating costs are.

Estimating and Controlling Expenses

Business success requires sound money management. If you find you are not keeping track of your financial planning revenues and expenses daily, consider hiring a part-time bookkeeper or assistant to keep your accounting records up to date. The alternative is to rearrange your schedule, dedicate several hours each week to reviewing your accounts, and discipline yourself to collect receipts and input data into your accounting software system. Regularly review the estimated operating budget you created before starting your business, and compare your actual expenses to the estimates. Investigate major discrepancies and adjust your business plan or your spending habits.

To calculate your operating expenses, add up all of your fixed costs, such as rent, phone service, car payments, ongoing marketing expenses, and the cost of any equipment spread out over its expected working life. For instance, if your office rent is $1,000 per month and the lease is 48 months, include a fixed cost of $48,000 in your calculation. Next, add the ongoing expenses that are paid on a weekly or monthly basis, such as the purchase of office supplies, advertising, entertaining clients, cleaning services, memberships in associations, and so on. Include an extra amount (30 percent is safe) for emergencies or unforeseen expenses. Do not forget to add employee wages and benefits or payments for services such as tax preparation. Using all of this information, calculate how much money you need each month to cover your expenses. An accountant can help you create a detailed projection of your operating costs by month and year. *(The sample business plan on the companion CD includes a projected income and expense sheet.)*

Costs Checklist

Utilities:	
Gas	$
Electricity	$
Water	$
Sewage	$

Office:	
Supplies	$
Equipment leases	$
Postage	$
Rent	$

Insurance:	
Vehicle	$
Workers' Compensation	$
General liability	$
Health	$
Life/key person	$

Loans:	
Business	$
Vehicle	$
Equipment	$

Marketing:	
Business cards	$
Website	$
Yellow pages	$

Marketing (Cont'd):	
Mailings	$
Printed material	$

Cost of sales:	
Other	$

Dues:	
Licensing	$
Chamber of Commerce	$
Professional/legal	$
BNI	$
Other	$

Equipment maintenance:	
Computer	$
Printer/copier	$
Auto	$

Employee(s):	
Full time	$
Part-time	$

Cost of business:	
Safety	$
One-time costs	$
Other	$

The expense of operating your business should be borne by your clients. Figure your basic cost of doing business using some common calendar measure — monthly, quarterly, or annually. This gives you a rough operating figure, so you know how well your business is doing without having to stop and do a detailed analysis. If the operating figure is $5,000 a month, in a 30-day month, you must make roughly $167 per day to cover basic expenses. Keep this figure in mind. If you are regularly exceeding that amount, you do not have to worry. If you are constantly making less than that amount, you need to discover why and then adjust either your business model or your operating expenses. For example, you may not be charging enough for your hourly services to make ends meet; you may be spending more time on each account than you originally planned; or you may be taking on too many charity cases, friends, and relatives at discounted rates. If money is not coming in because you do not have enough customers, you will have to do more aggressive marketing or offer different services. When too many people come in for a first-time consultation and never return, it could mean that a competitor is charging lower prices or that you are not convincing clients they need your services. If you are working full time and charging as much as your market will bear, you may have to reduce your operating expenses by moving to a cheaper office or laying off an employee.

Controlling Costs

You can make your profit margin higher by keeping your expenses low. Here is a brief look at how you can control business expenses:

Large purchases

Buy necessary furnishings and equipment secondhand or deeply discounted. Repurpose items you already own to fit your needs. Instead of purchasing a new desk, use a table you have until you can afford to purchase a desk, or borrow items from friends and family. Look for closeout sales and liquidations. Often, just before a new model of computer comes out, electronics stores will cut the price of the existing model. You can search for these discounts online. Computer stores often sell used computers acquired when a large business updated its equipment, and electronics manufacturers sell refurbished computers. When you buy refurbished electronics, you can get many of the special features you want, such as a large memory, for less than half the price of a new computer.

Service staples

Some of the ongoing costs associated with financial planning services cannot be avoided. For example, if you are providing investment advice, you may need paid access to Bloomberg, a system that provides statistics and information on investments. Some financial planning software is sold on a subscription basis. You can cut costs on some service staples, such as office supplies. Save money by keeping an inventory of necessary supplies such as printer ink, paper, letterhead stationery, pens, folders, and paper clips. Regularly restock these items so you do not have to rush out in an emergency and pay a premium for an urgently needed item such as an ink cartridge. Buy from discount office supply stores online, which are often less expensive, even with shipping, than the bigger office supply store chains. Compare prices carefully — many stores have sale prices on a few items and then charge more for others.

One of the biggest expenses is printing letters, statements, and reports for clients. When you buy a printer, compare the prices of ink and toner cartridges and check how many printed sheets you will get from each cartridge. A more expensive printer could save a lot of money if it uses ink or toner efficiently. Avoid color printing when you can; produce professional-looking documents using a black-and-white laser printer and letterhead stationery. Compare the cost of printing color pages on your printer and having them printed in bulk at an office-supply store. Buy refilled ink and toner cartridges instead of new ones. Save on paper and postage by going paperless as much as possible; give your clients the option of receiving reports and statements by e-mail or logging in to an online account to view them. Reduce the amount of paper you use in your office by keeping records and documents on your computer (be sure to have a backup system, or store your files with an online service).

Balance the importance of maintaining a professional image with the expense of paper and printing. Instead of having your logo printed on cardboard report folders, use plain folders and printed adhesive labels. That way you can use the labels sparingly and easily produce folders as needed instead of having to order a large quantity at a time.

Services

The services of professionals such as attorneys and accountants may be necessary for your business, but you might be able to cut costs by doing some things yourself. If you cannot afford to hire a payroll service, purchase accounting software, keep the books yourself, and issue your own paychecks. Time equals money. You must calculate whether the amount of money you save by doing your own bookkeeping is greater than the amount of money you could earn if you spent that time meeting with clients or preparing reports.

Put together a team of professionals who charge by the hour when you need their services. Develop personal relationships with them so you can call them when you have a question without setting up a formal appointment. Instead of having a lawyer draft contracts and other legal documents, use templates to create your own and then pay a lawyer to review them. Some of these professionals eventually may refer clients to you. You also might be able to barter your services in exchange for theirs.

Maintenance costs

Your operational costs include the maintenance of your office, equipment, company vehicles, and other machines you may own or lease for the business. These costs may include repair costs or regular servicing to keep everything in working order. Paying for regular maintenance can save you money by preventing damage that requires expensive repairs or replacement of equipment.

Utilities

Whether you run your financial planning business at another location or in your home, water and electricity are necessary operational costs. If you are running the business from its own location, the cost of utilities probably will be higher than the small increase in your bills when you run your business out of your home. Other utility costs include telephone and Internet service. You can keep costs down by subscribing only to those services necessary to run your business. For example, phone service packages may include many features you do not need. Check with the phone company to see how much you can save if you only have the features you need, such as call waiting and voice mail service.

Operating an energy-efficient business also saves money on utility bills. Turn off machines, equipment, and lights when they are not in use and unplug them from the power source. When you close your business for the day, make sure you turn everything off. If you leave your computer for more than ten minutes, place it in sleep mode or set it up so that it automatically goes into sleep mode after a specified amount of time.

Miscellaneous costs

Other costs you need to consider and be aware of include:

Labor taxes

If you have employees on your payroll, you are responsible for paying taxes to the state and federal governments. Payment of labor taxes requires you to establish an account with your business banking institution to deposit withholding amounts for each payroll period. These taxes typically include state and federal unemployment and social security.

Repair costs

Keep a cushion of extra cash on hand to cover the costs of unexpected repairs to equipment, a company vehicle, or your office building. A serious emergency could suddenly arise if a computer is infected by a virus or your hard drive crashes when you are preparing reports for a client deadline. You need to be able to take care of a situation like that immediately so you can continue with your work.

Client entertainment

There will be times when you want to impress your clients with a nice lunch, dinner, or tickets to the local sports game. Build some money into your budget to cover these types of client entertainment expenses. Keep track of your spending because most of these items are tax deductible.

Advertising

Marketing and promoting your business typically require a substantial budget — especially when you first launch the business. Regular advertising makes your business visible to prospective clients and brings in new business. If nobody knows your business exists, you will not attract clients and stay in business. Evaluate your advertising expenditures carefully and weed out those that do not seem to bring results. Look for advertising that brings you a high return on investment (ROI). A small inexpensive ad in a local school newsletter might be more effective in reaching your clients than an expensive quarter-page spread in the city newspaper.

Association dues and trade organizations

Many financial planning businesses pay trade dues or business association fees. Membership in a trade association increases your credibility and may include valuable benefits such as group health insurance or access to research data. Chamber of Commerce and business association meetings provide opportunities to network with other professionals who may become your clients.

Client costs

You may have extra expenses when you have to travel to meet with a client or book a meeting room. Whenever possible, the client should pay for costs of this nature as established in your written agreement, but you may need cash on hand to cover these expenses until you are reimbursed by the client.

Bad debt

Although you do everything in your power to avoid it, there will be times when a client goes bad or takes a wrong turn. A client may disappear without paying you everything he or she owes, or you may underestimate the time it takes to complete a job, which would result in cost overruns. Some business losses may be tax deductible, but they come directly out of your budget, so keep track of them.

The interest you pay on business credit card balances is not tax-deductible. If you use credit cards to make up for a shortfall and carry large credit card balances, you are probably paying high interest rates. All of the interest you are paying cannot be written off as a business expense at the end of the year.

Evaluating your progress

Once you establish a running tab of your income and your expenses, you can calculate your profit (or loss) by subtracting all of your costs and expenses from the total amount of money your services have brought into the company (revenue) over a specified period. If the resulting number is positive, you have a profit; if the number is negative, you have a loss. When you begin making a profit, decide how much of the company profit you will use to pay yourself a salary and how much of the profit will be reinvested in the business. For example, assume you are calculating profit and loss for the month of February, and the total monthly expenses are $2,575 with a total monthly income of $5,250.

Monthly profit: $5,250 − $2,575 = $2,675

Re-evaluating your business on a monthly or quarterly basis helps you focus on what you are doing so you can make corrections when necessary. You can use your software accounting program to produce reports and charts that show how your business is doing and where your money is going. You might learn from these reports that your monthly income consistently falls short of your target. Then you could look for places to cut costs — perhaps you are spending excessively on advertising or on client lunches. If you feel these expenses are necessary, you could consider raising your fees slightly to cover them.

Taxes

For a business owner, taxes are a year-round concern. The IRS requires business owners to maintain financial records for their businesses and to file receipts, invoices, and other records of expenses. These records serve more than one purpose: They are often useful for troubleshooting conflicts and discrepancies, proving that payments have been made, and maintaining peace of mind. You also save time by having financial data and records at your fingertips whenever you need them throughout the year. The recordkeeping system creates a paper trail of your business performance. The Internal Revenue Service (IRS) regularly reviews income and expense patterns and may require you to turn over your financial records for an audit if any anomalies are detected.

File federal, state, and local taxes on a timely basis. In some locations, you may be required to collect sales tax on services and periodically make payments to a governing body. Contact your city or state tax department for information about required licenses or tax filings and how and when to file. Most taxing entities now allow you to file and pay taxes online using simple procedures. You also can make payments by mail or in person.

Calculating Your Fees

As described in Chapter 1, financial planners follow a variety of business models, including charging flat fees for specific services, charging by the hour, charging a small percentage of the client's assets under management, and taking commissions on the sale of financial products. The fee-based model is becoming increasingly popular because clients believe the financial planner is putting their interests first instead of pushing the sales of particular financial products in order to earn commissions. Clients are willing to pay a percentage of their assets under management if they are confident the financial planner will do a good job of increasing their wealth.

You will occasionally under- or overprice services at the beginning, and there may be times when you find yourself working for nothing. You will know you have overpriced a service if customers keep going elsewhere. Keep track of what you estimate for which services and for which customers, and keep track of the outcome. Note when you succeed in selling a job and when you fail. Try to discover why the client decided to use, or not to use, your services — a polite question at the end of the interview will usually give you the answer. Go over your notes every week or two at first. Be aware of what you are doing, what works, what does not work, and what you might want to try differently.

It is common to require a prepayment for your services. If a comprehensive family plan costs $5,000, a portion of that (maybe $1,750) might have to be paid as a deposit before you begin work on the plan. Some planners charge a fee for an initial consultation and general advice. Others offer free initial consultations and charge only when the client engages their services. Some planners discreetly accept payments on a sliding scale for clients in financial difficulties.

Fee structures

You can charge clients two basic ways for your financial planning services. Each fee structure has advantages and disadvantages and is more appropriate for certain types of situations.

Flat fees

Although it is a relatively new concept in the financial planning business, many personal advisers now charge flat fees for their services. A flat fee can be an hourly rate or a menu of fees charged for specific services. For example, a financial planner might charge $3,750 to create and write a family financial plan.

The biggest disadvantage of an hourly rate is that clients may suspect you are taking longer than necessary to help them work through their problems or reach their goals in order to inflate your fees. Consciously or unconsciously, you may find yourself working more hours than necessary with a client to make enough money to cover your expenses. Charging hourly rates tends to pit the financial planner and the client against each other and can cause a rift between them. Some clients, however, prefer to have you work on an hourly basis.

It may take some trial and error to correctly price your hourly rate. If your hourly rate is too low, you may have to work long hours to make enough money to live on. If your hourly rate is too high, you may not be able to attract enough business. Gather information about the hourly rates of local financial advisers who charge by the hour. These figures probably will cover a wide range, and you can use a sliding scale to determine your own rates.

There are two other methods for calculating a range of possible hourly rates. One is to build your hourly rate from the bottom up. For example, if you were working as an employee for a company, you probably worked a set number of hours each pay period. Divide your salary by the number of hours to determine the hourly rate you are earning as an employee. Assume your weekly (gross) salary is $1,500, and you work 40 hours per week.

Hourly rate: $1,500 / 40 = $37.50

You need to charge your financial planning clients this base rate to make an income comparable to what you would make as a company employee. On top of this base rate, add the cost of your health insurance, retirement plan, and other expenses. Instead of $37.50 per hour, you may need to charge an hourly fee closer to $50 an hour in order to pay yourself and cover your business expenses.

Another approach to calculating your hourly fee is to build the rate per hour from the top down. Take the gross amount of money you need to earn each month and work your way down from this figure. For example, you know you need to bring in $10,000 per month, and you plan to work six eight-hour days per week. One hour of each day will be devoted to administrative tasks or marketing, so in one month you will do 168 hours of work. Divide the number of hours of work per month into the amount of money you want to make to determine your hourly rate.

Hourly rate: $10,000 / 168 = $59.52

No matter what method you use to calculate your hourly rate, the market must be able to support that dollar amount for your business to be profitable. A client who is convinced that you are the right person for the job is less likely to be concerned about what your hourly rate is (within reason, of course). Most businesses and clients assume they will pay 20 to 30 percent more than the standard going rate for a financial planner in order to receive a superior level of service. A client who believes you can provide superior service will not to mind paying a premium for it.

Commissions

The original source of income for financial advisers was commissions on the sale of financial products, such as mutual funds and life insurance policies. Many financial advisers still use this method, in which the financial adviser is paid a percentage of the amount of business the client does with the adviser. For example, if the commission is 5 percent and the client conducts $1 million worth of business with the financial adviser, the adviser earns a fee of $50,000.

Many financial advisers moved away from this fee structure because some clients felt advisers were pressuring them to buy products in an effort to increase commissions.

Client Contracts

After the initial consultation, provide the client with an accurate estimate of the costs of your services before asking him or her to sign a written agreement. There is no universal contract for personal financial planning agreements. Include all of the details in the contract, such as the length of the relationship, the cost, precisely what services you will provide, and the payment schedule. The contract should include a cancellation clause detailing the circumstances under which you or the client can cancel the contract and how a cancellation will be done. Customers always have a right to cancel a contract for nonperformance or, in most cases, general dissatisfaction.

Consult your attorney about your state's laws concerning cancellation of these types of contracts and the rights of each party. Contract requirements vary by state, and each state has its own requirements for terms of cancellation, conflict resolution, and so on. You can get information about contract law in your state from a lawyer, the local Chamber of Commerce or Better Business Bureau, your State Department of Development, or state attorney general's office.

Written contracts are essential. When you seal a deal with a verbal agreement, you have no recourse if your customer decides he or she does not like the work you have done or feels you have not fulfilled your obligations. You can bring action against him or her in small-claims court, but that costs money and time, and there is no guarantee that you will win the case.

Planning for profitability

Profitability is directly derived from how you price your services. A good strategy is to price your services in such a way that you remain competitive while still making a reasonable profit. It is better to make a reasonable profit with lower prices than to price yourself out of the market with charges that are too high. Therefore, take extreme care when pricing your services. Calculate your costs, estimate the tangible benefits to your customers, and compare your services and prices to your competitors in the financial planning market.

For example, suppose you calculate that you need $5,000 a month to cover your operating expenses. Assume you will work six days a week, at least in your first few months in business. Four weeks at six days per week or 24 working days during the month. Your daily earning requirement is $208, or $26 per hour for an eight-hour workday, just to meet your $5,000 monthly cost of doing business. (You might receive additional income from commissions on the sales of products to your clients.) A 50-hour workweek, for 50 weeks, gives you a total of 2,500 work hours, on average, per year, plus two weeks of vacation. Working the usual 40 hours per week totals only 2,000 hours, which means you have to make more per hour to cover operating expenses.

Remember, you will not be earning $26 every hour. To run your business, you must spend time on marketing, maintaining equipment, doing accounts and other "non-billable" work. This means your actual billable hours will total about 1,500 to 2,000 hours per year if you are working 50 hours each week, so for example, $40 per hour x 2,000 hours = annual income of $80,000. This $80,000 has to cover all those expenses you previously identified. If you want to make a profit, you will have to earn more than that amount.

As an independent businessperson, you are responsible for your own health insurance, vacation pay, retirement savings, and taxes. You need to take into account the total cost of living for you and your family, plus all business expenses and overhead.

Evaluating the competition

The personal financial planning business tends to be competitive. How can you keep up with what your rivals are doing, where they are doing it, how well they do it, and what they charge?

One way is to attend local professional group events. By listening to the conversations of your associates and peers at luncheons or seminars hosted by your area Chamber of Commerce, or a local Rotary chapter or business association, you can get a good understanding of the local economic climate. You can gather information by interviewing your suppliers and customers. Always be polite and professional. Do not speak negatively about your competitor in public, even if you are many times more experienced and qualified than the person you are criticizing. Just emphasize what you do best and ignore what the competition does.

Do not charge what your competition is charging without checking to see that it covers your overhead and generates a profit. Perhaps your competition is losing money. Your competitors have different cost structures. Your prices should be based on your overhead, your employees, and your profit goals.

A look at national average prices for services may give you a general idea of what to charge, though prices vary a great deal from one location to another.

National average prices are updated annually in various publications such as Costhelper® (**www.costhelper.com/cost/finance/financial-planner.html**) and Payscale.com (**www.payscale.com/research/US/Job=Personal_Financial_Advisor/Salary**). The U.S. Bureau of Labor Statistics also tracks information about a number of workforce and industry segments in its *Occupational Outlook Handbook* (**www.bls.gov/oco**).

CHAPTER 8

Marketing Your Financial Planning Business

As a personal financial planner, you are selling yourself, your experience, and the services you provide. Centering on your unique skills and qualities, you must create a public image, or brand, for your business that conveys your values, personality, and character to potential clients. Your slogan, marketing materials, and the look of your office should reflect how you want your target audience to feel when they see your business card, website, or logo. Your brand should be consistently evident throughout your business in your attitude and the attitude of your staff, the décor in your office, your ads, printed materials, and your activities in the community.

Your brand provides a focus for all of your marketing efforts and everything you do to attract attention to your business: flyers, business cards, ads, billboards, direct mail, website, and your presence at public events. In the beginning, your goal will be to attract potential clients to your office by creating widespread awareness of your business in the community and to convert those potential clients into loyal customers. Once you have a base of established customers, you will still need to continue regular advertising, but you can rely on word-of-mouth referrals and your reputation to bring in new business.

Character

The first step in creating your "brand" is to determine the character of your company. As a planning business, how should the business feel and act? What does the business like, and what does it dislike? What type of clients will it be serving, and what are their likes and dislikes? A financial planner catering to families with special-needs children will want to create a warm, light-hearted, caring atmosphere. A planner who manages the investments of wealthy retired businessmen needs to project dignity, prosperity, respect, and self-possession. Make a list of adjectives that describe the feelings you want your clients to have about your business.

Aesthetics

The visual components of branding include your logo, character or mascot, color schemes, and font styles. In branding a company, it is important that the look of your visual components matches the way you want customers to feel about your company. Write down your ideas about how the values, morals, strengths, and benefits of your planning business can be reflected in a company logo, colors, font styles, and other representations.

Visual branding works in two ways: whenever existing clients see these visual representations of the company, such as on an envelope or a sign, their feelings about working with your business are reinforced. Prospective clients who see these visual representations may be intrigued and want to learn more about your company or be turned off by what they see and move on. These visual symbols should trigger an instant recognition of your business in prospective and current clients. The purpose of branding is to create both a subconscious and a conscious connection between your financial planning business and the people, businesses, or organizations that can benefit from your services.

Branding is Perception

Sometimes a branding effort does not succeed in conveying the desired public image. A "brand" is how current and potential customers really perceive a company, rather than how the company wants to be perceived. Successful branding aligns public perception of a company with the image it is trying to portray.

Three ways to balance the brand with audience perception

1. Create and write a mission statement for your company that is easily understandable and memorable.

2. Survey potential and current clients to see what they think your company does and what services it offers. If their answers match the purpose of the company as expressed in its mission statement, the brand and brand perception are in balance. If not, adjustments need to be made.

Target different segments of your audience with different messages while conveying the same core values. Any financial planning business caters to several market segments, such as different age groups or people in different stages of their economic lives. Create separate messages to target each of these audiences. Design your website with special sections for each of your target audiences. Create a series of newspaper and Internet ads that appeal to families with young children who want to plan for the future and another series for retirees who need to manage fixed incomes and plan their estates. Place each series of ads on websites and in publications where they will be seen by the appropriate age group, and direct them to the corresponding sections of your website.

Weaving the Brand Together

Once you determine the look and feel that best represents your personal and company brand, weave it into every aspect of your financial planning business. Branding encompasses everything related to your company, internal or external. The same standards apply whether you are sending out an internal memo to your employees or e-mail to your client list.

Your brand should be evident in your:

- Company logo
- Business cards
- E-mail signature
- Letterhead
- Brochures
- Marketing kit
- Website
- Blog
- Mailing envelopes
- Promotional items, such as pens, magnets, notepads, and drink cozies

- Proposals
- Client agreements or contracts
- Color scheme and office decor

Marketing Messages

A marketing message is the signal you want to send to your current and potential customers about your services. Some marketing professionals refer to this as a positioning statement because it is a written statement that "positions" your company and how you want to come across to clients. For example, as a financial planner, you might want to convey that you are honest, knowledgeable, trustworthy, and put the best interests of your clients ahead of profit. Or you might want to emphasize that your clients' financial futures are safe in your hands.

After you have defined your essential positioning statement in order, establish one to three key messages you want to send to current and potential customers through your marketing efforts. These key marketing messages directly promote the products or services you are touting for your business, but they are not taglines or memorable and catchy phrases. They are the messages you want the audience to walk away with after reading your marketing material.

List the three primary services you plan to offer your clients. Under each service, write out how the service benefits clients. Now, form messages about the services and benefits that you want clients to understand when they are exposed to your marketing initiatives.

Logo

Your company logo is a visual symbol that instantly identifies your business. Make sure it features prominently in your ads and on your website, business cards, stationery and documents. You can put your logo on items such as pens and coffee mugs that you distribute to potential customers, so it becomes a familiar sight.

Business cards

Business cards are a marketing essential for a financial planner. You will need them to hand out at networking events, give to clients and contacts when you introduce yourself, and insert in the marketing kit you send to prospective clients. You can place small stands with your business cards on counters in print shops and other stores where your potential clients might pick them up. Many of your prospective clients will not need your services immediately; they will put your business card away in a wallet or handbag and remember you when they do need assistance.

Your business cards should be of a quality that reflects your business standards but not too expensive because you need so many of them. You can hire a graphic designer to design your business cards and then send the file to a printer to have the cards printed, but there are many less expensive alternatives. You can order professionally printed business cards online from websites such as Vistaprint (**www.vistaprint.com**) and 48hourprint. com® (**www.48hourprint.com**). These sites have professionally designed business card templates that you can customize and personalize, or you can upload your own design.

Desktop publishing programs also have templates for business cards you can print on your own printer using business card stock purchased at an office supply or stationery store. This is probably the least expensive way to get business cards, but it takes time and may cheapen the image of your company.

Website

A business website is another marketing essential. Prospective clients will visit your website to learn about your services and pricing before they make an appointment for an initial consultation. Your existing clients may refer their friends to your website and will go there to look up your address and contact information when they forget your telephone number. Your business website can be a simple overview of your business with contact information and an e-mail link, or you can create a dynamic website that you update regularly with financial news, a blog, and current information for your clients. Some financial planners conduct part of their business online by having clients log in and viewing reports and investment accounts whenever they want.

You can build and maintain your own website, hire a website designer to create the site and teach you to maintain it, or hire a professional company to build and maintain it for you. It costs little to purchase a domain name and set up your own website using a template and the free design software available from companies such as GoDaddy.com (**www.godaddy.com**), Wix.com (**www.wix.com**), Buildfree.org (**www.buildfree.org**), and Weebly.com (**www.weebly.com**). You can also design your own website with a desktop publishing or design program such as Microsoft Publisher or Adobe® Dreamweaver®. Website hosting can cost from $4.95 per month to about $50 per month, depending on the hosting service and the amount of memory and number of e-mail addresses.

Large Web design companies may charge thousands of dollars for their services, but you should be able to find a smaller company or individual who will design your website for $200 to $400. The designer may also charge you for making changes to the site after it is up and running. You can either write the text (content) for the site yourself or hire a writer to do it — the cost depends on the amount of content. Companies like Smarsh® (**www.financialvisions.com**), Advisor Resources (**http://advisorresources.net**) and Financial Advisor Website Design (**http://financialadvisorwebsitedesign.com**) offer hosting with customized design packages with special features for financial planners, such as financial news feeds, stock market data, client access pages and financial glossaries, for a monthly fee. All you have to do is regularly add personal touches, such as blog posts, and upload your client data. In addition, these companies make sure that your website is compliant with SEC and FINRA security standards for websites that sell financial products or gather personal information from clients.

Responsible internet usage

NASD (National Association of Securities Dealers) and FINRA (Financial Industry Regulatory Authority) have developed a series of rules concerning the advertisement and sale of financial products and services over the Internet. These rules prohibit finance professionals from making exaggerated claims, omitting information about the risk associated with specific investments, or promising or predicting investment results. There are also strict rules governing the use of e-mail, blog posts, and electronic social media to recommend or sell investments. You can learn more about these rules in the *Guide to the Internet for Registered Representatives* on the FINRA website (**www.finra.org/industry/issues/advertising/p006118**).

As a small business, you are responsible for protecting your clients' personal and financial information. The widespread use of wireless technology and electronic devices to access information over the Internet, as well as the ease with which laptop computers can be carried around, makes sensitive data vulnerable to theft.

You must protect your computers from hackers and identity thieves and to restrict employee access to sensitive files and information. Steps recommended by the National Institute of Standards and Technology include:

- Protect information and networks from viruses, spyware, and other malicious code.
- Have a secure Internet connection.

- Install software firewalls to protect your business computers from hackers.

- Regularly update security software.

- Make backup copies of important business information.

- Restrict access to your business computers and networks, and lock up laptops when not in use.

- Secure your wireless network so outsiders cannot access it.

- Train your employees in basic security procedures.

- Require individual password-protected user accounts for each employee on business computers.

- Limit employee access to data and information.

- Destroy the hard drives when you dispose of old computers.

You will find helpful suggestions in the NIST publication *Small Business Information Security: The Fundamentals* (**http://csrc.nist.gov/publications/nistir/ir7621/nistir-7621.pdf**).

If your clients' personal information is compromised in any way, you will be responsible for notifying them and could be liable if they consequently become victims of identity theft. It is much easier to prevent this from happening by practicing basic security procedures than to try to undo the damage after it occurs.

Planning your website design

Before you begin speaking with website designers, have a clear concept of how you want your website to look and function. A website designer will be guided by your vision; his or her job is to provide the technical and artistic expertise. Spend some time exploring the websites of other financial planning companies and your local competitors. Observe how each website is organized, where the navigation menus are located, and the ease with which you can find information. Note the way in which information is presented, the use of videos, and the color schemes. Look for features and functions you want to include in your own website.

The overall design of your website should reflect the unique qualities of your business. Your input is important, but your personal tastes and preferences might not be the most effective. For example, you might want to your website to open with an impressive animation using Adobe Flash®, a multimedia platform that allows streaming of audio and video. However, visitors to your site probably want to access information as quickly as possible and may not be able to view the Flash presentation clearly on a handheld device or an older computer. A plain home page in soft colors with a clear message may produce better results and encourage visitors to view more pages on your website. An experienced website designer knows how to appeal to an audience and how to make the website easy for visitors to use. Website designers also understand how to optimize your website (SEO — search engine optimization), so it is found easily by Internet search engines. Including important keywords in the first paragraphs of text on your homepage, adding metatags and descriptions, and having multiple sites link to yours will help increase traffic to your site. Listen to the suggestions of the website designer before you decide on a final design.

The sections and pages you need for your website will depend on its purpose and the business activities for which it will be used. Make a list of all the things you want your website to do — this is known as the "scope" of your project. A website designer needs this list to prepare a proposal and a price quote. Your primary purpose is to promote your business. To accomplish this, you must provide your logo, address, and contact information; your résumé and certifications; and a description of your services. In addition, you might want to display client testimonials or financial news and information, collect e-mail addresses for a monthly newsletter, or provide clients with personalized pages where they can view information about their accounts. Your plans for maintaining and updating your website are also part of its scope.

Your website should be created so you or someone on your staff can add new pages, edit text, update each section, maintain blogs and newsletters, change photos, and manage sales and reports without having to rely on the Web designer. Make this clear in your Web design contract, and define exactly what kind of ongoing maintenance the Web designer will provide and the procedures for making changes to the website design.

Home page

Your home page is both a snapshot of your entire website and a statement about your business. In a few seconds, someone who opens your home page will understand what kind of services you offer and what information is available on your website. Your home page should be exciting and informative. The top portion of your home page, which appears in the browser screen when someone opens your website, is the most important because many readers will not stay on your website if they do not see something that interests them right away. According to Nielsen Online, the average time spent looking at a Web page is 56 seconds. You have less than a minute to grab a prospective client's attention.

At a glance, a visitor to your home page should see your name and logo, a marketing message, and a list of the sections of your website. Detailed descriptions, pricing information, résumés, and mission statements can be placed on other pages or in a lower section of the home page and linked to an introductory sentence or navigation bar at the top of the home page.

Navigation

Navigation refers to the way in which visitors to your website move from one page to another. A navigation menu across the top or down the side of your home page links your visitors to the various sections of your website. Website designers know that a certain percentage of visitors leave a site each time they are required to click on a button or link to open another page. It is important to organize your website so your visitors quickly find what they are looking for and are able to return easily to pages they have already looked at. Divide the functions of your website into distinct sections: an area for prospective clients, an area for existing clients, an area for financial news and data, and so on.

About us

Most business websites have an "About Us" section with information about the company, a mission statement, and anything else that the company wants to communicate officially to the public. This is a good place to put your résumé and the skills and qualifications of your staff. This section might also include links to your contact information or marketing kits.

Marketing kits

Your entire marketing kit (which will be further explained later in this chapter) should be contained in the pages of your website. It is a good idea to provide a printable version of your marketing kit that clients can print and show to their families or bring with them when they come to their first appointment. They might want to ask you about certain services or features. Your URL on your business cards, letterhead and e-mail signature directs people to your website, where they can find detailed information about your company.

Community

You might want to encourage your clients to become involved in an online community by posting comments in a blog or message board and signing up for social media. For example, if you are serving families with special-needs children, you could host a blog where they can post comments about their concerns and experiences. Never allow posts to appear on your blog site without first being reviewed and approved by someone in your company. Most blogs have a feature that requires you to approve a message or comment before it can be published. You do not want a disgruntled client to post negative comments about your company or someone with a political agenda to post inflammatory statements. Keep your blog focused on your business with posts that encourage or enlighten your clients.

A community section can contain information about charities and benefit performances or general news items about finance. When visitors to your website are allowed to contribute to an online community and interact with other visitors, they develop a stronger trust in your company.

Other Forms of Online Marketing

A website is not the only form of online marketing available. With the advances in social media, it is easier and more cost effective than ever to get your message out to your potential customers. Here are some potential vessels that could carry your advertisements and news.

Twitter

Some financial planners use Twitter (**http://twitter.com**) to send their clients reminders and updates and recommend relevant news articles. Your clients may or may not want to receive regular news flashes and reminders depending on the types of services you offer and how involved they are in managing their own accounts. Some of your clients are already active on Twitter. Establish yourself on Twitter and invite them to follow you, so that they will receive the "tweets," or posts, you put online. Sending out regular tweets reinforces your image as a source of sound financial advice. These clients will remember you when they or their friends need a financial planner. Twitter can also help you expand your potential client base. To get an idea of what other financial planners are "tweeting," look at AdvisorTweets™ (**www.advisortweets.com**), a collection of tweets from financial advisers.

CASE STUDY:
USE TWITTER TO EXPAND
YOUR CLIENT BASE

TJ Gilsenan
Present and founder
The Interactive Advisor
http://theinteractiveadvisor.com

TJ Gilsenan is president and founder of The Interactive Advisor, a firm dedicated to helping independent advisers better use Web marketing in their practices. A former financial adviser, he has been helping Independent Advisors grow their businesses for almost 20 years.

This is an excerpt from his article, "Why Twitter Matters to a Financial Advisor," posted on *Financial Planning.com* (**www.financial-planning.com**) on March 4, 2011.

"Twitter gives you an opportunity to develop a following of your own outside your client base. These people may someday become new clients! Here are a few ways to attract more quality, and qualified, followers:

Participate in the conversation. Become a part of your industry on Twitter. Learn what other financial advisors are "tweeting" and what kind of language they are using. Start by looking at AdvisorTweets — an aggregated, curated collection of what financial advisors say on Twitter.

Follow people that you want to know. Follow people that you are interested in and that you want to attract, such as industry experts and potential leads. Connect with me on Twitter @TJ_Gilsenan.

Introduce yourself. Social media is like one big cocktail party. If there are people that you are really focused on getting to know, introduce yourself. A personal introduction is easy and effective. You can also make a comment about their blog or ask a question.

Stay focused. If you are on Twitter for business, keep it industry focused. Although some personal interaction is acceptable, discussing relevant financial topics will attract a more targeted audience.

Do not rely solely on automation. If you use automation tools (e.g. Facebook status posted directly to Twitter), make sure you create pertinent messages and schedule posts over a varied period. Automated only posts can look very impersonal and be seen as SPAM.

Tweet a balanced mix of information. Include content from your blog as well as your thoughts on market news or links to interesting articles.

Join Twitter discussions. Get involved in discussions about financial topics to draw attention to your expertise. Use the Twitter search tool or search by hashtag (#retirement planning, #stockmarket, #financial) to find relevant topics.

Retweet (RT). Retweet posts that you find interesting to increase your visibility. People who follow the person you Retweet or the hashtag you include will see you as someone with similar interests. Make sure you use the @name when you mention other Twitter users to help build relationships. If others are monitoring conversations about themselves, they will notice your Retweet.

Listen to your audience. Pay attention to what your audience is talking about. What questions are they asking? What information are they requesting? If you provide valuable Tweets to your followers, you will likely attract more quality followers. Respond to questions with quality content and people will see you as an informative resource, follow your Tweets, and may even Retweet you.

Promote your Twitter handle. Add your handle (your @name) to your e-mail signature, business cards, website contact information and your blog."

You can learn more about marketing your business with the Internet and social media on Gilsenan's website, The Interactive Advisor (**http://theinteractiveadvisor.com**).

E-mail newsletter

E-mail is a powerful way to communicate with clients and generate new business. Encourage new clients and visitors to your website to add their e-mail addresses to your address list, and send out newsletters at regular intervals informing them about new financial products, changes in tax laws and government regulations, and other news that might be of interest. A regular e-mail keeps your company's name fresh in the minds of clients. E-mail recipients often forward interesting newsletters to their friends and family. You also can use your e-mail list to learn about your client base by documenting their responses to special offers and invitations and their use of coupons.

Blogs, podcasts, and webinars

Attract the attention of potential clients by offering free financial advice in regular newsletters, blogs, recorded podcasts, and live webinars offered over the Internet. Some groups of people, particularly young professionals, actively use social media for every aspect of their lives. Older retirees may be less computer savvy and prefer e-mail or more traditional styles of communication. Get to know your clients and the types of media they use, and then develop a communication network that will appeal to them.

Posting interesting articles regularly on your blog and on personal finance discussion boards and blogs will attract traffic to your website and help build your reputation. Articles do not have to be lengthy. Two paragraphs on a topic currently in the news or an issue that affects your clients are enough. It is important to post consistently in order to attract a regular readership. Writing takes time. Decide how much time you can afford to set aside every week or month for writing articles and updating your blog, and plan an appropriate publicity campaign. Send updates out to your e-mail list with links to your latest article. Include your Web address and an invitation to your blog on your business card and in any print ads. Contact your local newspaper to see if it would be interested in publishing your monthly article or including a link to your blog on its website.

Some financial planners build a reputation by giving money management seminars and talks to local organizations and schools. You can take this one step further by making video recordings of your lectures and putting them on your website. You can make your videos available to a wider audience by uploading them on sites such as YouTube (**www.youtube.com**) and linking to them from your website. Podcasting is the creation of audio or video files that can be downloaded by your listeners to their computers or MP3 players and listened to at their convenience. For example, your clients could listen to your lectures while driving or working out at the gym. Programs to make audio and video recordings and create MP3 files often are included in camera software and many standard computer packages. Free software to record and encode podcasts is available from Audacity® (**http://audacity.sourceforge.net**) and LAME (**http://lame.sourceforge.net/index.php**). There are many inexpensive programs, such as a $70 audio podcasting package by RecordForAll (**www.recordforall.com**), that are easy to use and allow you to produce high-quality audio lectures.

RSS (Really Simple Syndication) feeds allow your clients to subscribe to your blog or lecture series and automatically receive updates whenever you post new material. You can develop a program to coach your clients, inform them of new developments, and remind them when it is time to prepare for taxes.

You also can hold online meetings or classes using videoconferencing services. Send out e-mails inviting your clients to register to participate in scheduled classes. Free classes and question-and-answer sessions are a good way to build client loyalty, but you also can charge fees for useful training seminars. GoToWebinar® (**www.gotomeeting.com/fec**) allows you to conduct unlimited online seminars for as little as $99 per month. An annual plan with iLinc® (**www.ilinc.com**) costs as little as $79 per month. If you can generate enough interest among your clients, videoconferencing is a relatively inexpensive way to generate publicity for your business.

Branding on the Internet

Websites, blogs, and social media networks present entirely new branding and marketing opportunities. Clients in their 60s and younger are likely to make extensive use of the Internet when researching businesses and deciding whether to use a financial planner. The youngest generations are strongly influenced by electronic media and social networking. Highly educated clients will expect to have access to you online. Do not miss an opportunity to promote your business through electronic media.

Be search-engine friendly

Controlling your branding message is as important online as it is offline because most potential customers use Internet search engines to find information about companies, products, services, and people. You can expand your message online by contributing articles and blog posts to websites dealing with finance and linking them to your business website. When writing material for the company website or posting blogs and articles online, include keywords that customers would type to find the services your financial planning company provides.

Register your URLs

Gain control of your business name by registering it as a domain name (website address), along with at least the top five variations. Variations may include the .com, .net, and .us extensions of the domain name or other variations such as the business name spelled out completely, the business name acronym, or common misspellings. If your financial planning business does not include your name, for example, you may also wish to purchase your personal name as a domain name. It costs only about $10 to register a domain name for a year. Each of your URLs can be linked to your website. Having your business name as your URL helps potential clients find you online.

Write and post with care

Be careful what you say when you post something online. When you write and publish something online, it instantly disseminates around the world. What you write should reflect your financial planning business's mission statement and shed a positive light on your business.

Because your financial planning business centers on you and your skills, your brand extends beyond your business website to your personal profiles on social networking sites such as Facebook and MySpace. Avoid posting racy photos of yourself or political or potentially problematic personal statements online. Like it or not, your life is no longer private. You do not want potential clients to see anything online that might make them mistrust you.

Be consistent

Branding requires consistency. The same colors, logo, look, and feel should run through all of your marketing material — website, e-mail, online banner ads, print ads, letterhead, brochures, and business cards.

Printed Marketing Materials

Although the Internet increasingly predominates as a source of information, in many situations you will need printed materials to give to clients and advertise your business. You now have many inexpensive choices, such as brochures printed at a local office supply store or business service, but certain groups of clients will be impressed by high-quality letterhead stationery and glossy brochures. Be sensitive to your clients when designing printed materials.

Brochures and one-sheets

Company brochures promoting your services and giving your contact information are used for various marketing initiatives. They can be handed out at trade shows, included in marketing kits to media professionals or potential clients, and displayed in places where clients might pick them up. You can hire a graphic designer to design a traditional full-color brochure and have several thousand copies printed, but there is no need to spend a lot of money on brochures that you might not use before they become outdated. Your computer and graphic design software allow you the flexibility to print customized brochures as you need them. Have the graphic designer make you some brochure templates with areas you can edit or insert text. You can print small quantities on your printer, or give the file to a local printer or office supply store on a CD or by e-mail and order a few hundred copies. When you move to a new address, or add a new service or financial product, you easily can bring your brochure up to date.

Vistaprint (**www.vistaprint.com**) and 48hourprint.com (**www.48hourprint. com**) allow you to design your own brochure, add the content, and print the quantity you need. You also can upload your own brochure design to one of these websites to print.

Marketing kits

A service-based financial planning business must make a good impression on potential clients. A marketing kit provides your audience with more information than is possible to fit on a business card or in a brochure — or what you could say in an elevator pitch (a one-minute sales talk that can be delivered during a brief social encounter).

Marketing kits can be a powerful sales tool; leave the kit as a takeaway from a client meeting, or drop it in the mail as a follow-up to a phone conversation or in response to an e-mail request for more information from a prospective client. Always include two business cards and a company brochure if you have one. A marketing kit typically includes:

Folder

You need a folder or some sort of holder for the marketing kit. The folder should look professional because it is the first impression your prospect receives. Have folders professionally printed with your company name and logo, or affix a printed adhesive label to a plain linen pocket folder.

Marketing template

A marketing template is the layout for each piece of the marketing kit. It might be simple letterhead stationery, or it might be composed of several pages with your logo incorporated in a graphic design. The written text on each page can be edited to appeal to a specific client, or you can print a number of standard pages and select those most appropriate for the client.

USP

Earlier in this book, you learned about creating a unique selling proposition to make your financial planning business stand out from competitors. Your USP is a central theme of your marketing kit. Word it so it shows how your company can benefit your customers from the customer's point of view, and feature it in all your marketing materials.

Sell the benefits

Many financial planning businesses provide a list of features rather than pointing out the benefits a client enjoys by working with their companies. When you list a financial planning service in your marketing kit, also explain how this service benefits the client.

Service offering

Include a bulleted list of your services that can be reviewed with a quick glance. Follow the bulleted list with a more descriptive list of the financial planning services offered by your company.

Testimonials

Client testimonials can sell your services better than anything you can say to prospects. Include a full page of client testimonials, or have your clients record testimonials that you can include on a DVD or CD as part of the marketing kit.

Articles or media coverage

Third-party endorsements from the media should be included in the marketing kit. Include reprints of articles published about your company; DVDs of media interviews; or clips of newspaper, magazine, or online articles where you have been quoted as an expert source or your financial planning business is mentioned.

Personal and Company Image

A professional image and reputation are important in a financial planning business. Clients value ethical behavior and trustworthiness; while missed appointments and work that is incomplete or of poor quality leave clients with a bad impression. Most individuals and corporate employees refer businesses that have done a good job for them, so make a good impression the first time.

Dress and act in a professional manner

No matter how brilliant you are in financial matters, if you show up for a meeting in wrinkled clothes with disheveled hair and a coffee stain on your shirt, you will not make a favorable impression. Dress appropriately and be well groomed. Avoid using foul language or behaving rudely. Work on correcting bad habits and curbing negative personality traits — even if you have to create a work persona you put on when you talk to clients on the phone or walk into an office for a meeting.

Create a professional image

- Minimize any negative aspects that could be misconstrued as unprofessional, such as body language or appearance.

- Be straightforward with clients. They will respect you if you let them know what you can and cannot do and are honest about their needs and your ability to fulfill them.

- Dress professionally. Wear what you would expect the client to be wearing or something even better. If you look sloppy, clients will believe your work is sloppy and may decide not to work with you.

- Under-promise and over-deliver. Do not make promises you cannot keep. Always clearly state what you can and cannot do. It is better to tell a client that something cannot be done and then achieve it for them than to tell them you can do something and not deliver the desired results.

- Connect your personal image with the business's image by handing out business cards, memos, and report covers with your company logo and branding whenever appropriate.

Building Your Reputation

The two biggest contributors to the reputation of a financial planner are the quality of his or her work and how well the financial adviser presents him or herself in public. It is easier to build and maintain a good reputation than to overcome a bad one. Once your reputation is damaged, you have to work doubly hard to regain your clients' confidence in the future, and you may never fully recover.

Build a positive reputation quickly by always performing your tasks and completing client interactions to the best of your ability. Financial planning is your passion and area of expertise; make yourself readily available and easy to talk to, and keep lines of communication open with your clients.

Community involvement also helps boost your reputation. Volunteering and working in the community not only shows you in a good light, but it brings you into personal contact with many people who could become clients or refer business to you. Support a favorite cause by offering your services pro bono to nonprofit organizations. Give a free seminar through the Chamber of Commerce to teach local businesses how to reduce tax obligations or through a church to teach families how to plan for college. Write and submit news pieces, editorials, or articles that give a unique and interesting perspective on finance to local newspapers and to magazines within your field. For example, as a financial adviser, offer a piece on debt management to a family magazine. Write a book on an aspect of your job and career, and promote it at meetings and conferences.

Any encounter with a member of the community could result in a new client for your business. When you are chatting with another volunteer parent during an elementary school function, sitting next to a businessman at a Chamber of Commerce luncheon, or visiting your great-aunt in a nursing home, you may be speaking to someone who can refer a client. Always be polite and friendly, mention your business in a casual way, and try to steer the conversation towards some topic that involves financial planning. Listen carefully to what people say, and they will open up about their concerns. When someone likes you and feels sympathetic towards you, he or she is likely to think of a friend or family member who needs your services and remember you later. Any situation can become a marketing opportunity.

CHAPTER 9

Winning and Retaining Clients

Your marketing efforts make the community aware of your existence and bring prospective clients to your door. The essence of your business however, is getting those prospects to sign a contract and then giving them the best service possible. The key is effective communication with your client before, during, and after your relationship begins.

Communication includes both the verbal and written interchanges you will have with your client. Fortunately, effective communication skills can be learned. If you do not already possess a natural gift for communication, with practice you gradually will develop your abilities to understand a client's concerns and address them in a way that he or she can understand.

Written Communication (Before the Relationship)

Written communication is just as important as verbal communication. Putting information in writing helps you clarify and organize your thoughts and avoids problems and misunderstandings later.

Six Essential Methods of Communication

Six aspects of communication are particularly important for financial advisers:

1: Carefully choose your words

Often, what you have to say to a client is not as important as *how* you say it. Think about what you are going to say before you speak. Once you know what you need to say, make sure you word it in a way that does not sound negative, combative, or give the wrong impression to the client. For example, rather than saying, "You are doing it incorrectly," say something less abrasive, such as, "Have you ever approached it like this…?"

You are saying essentially the same thing without attacking the client.

2: Ask questions first

Gathering information from the client at the beginning of the project sets the stage for the rest of the project. Never make assumptions about clients or what they already have tried to do on their own before hiring you as a financial adviser. Jumping in with suggestions before first asking the right questions may result in embarrassment. Gather all of the facts before you determine what the client expects from working with you.

When you ask questions, listen carefully to the client's responses. A client's words and mannerisms provide many clues to what he or she really means. Rather than formulating what you are going to say next while the client is talking, make an effort to understand fully what the client is saying. Repeat what you have understood back to the client to make sure you have it right.

Most clients are more than willing to answer your questions, but some may be resistant or self-conscious about giving truthful answers. When you perceive that a client is resisting giving full answers to your questions, explain that there are several different ways to accomplish his or her goal and that your questions are meant to clarify the situation to make sure you implement the most effective strategy.

3: Be enthusiastic

Each client believes that his or her financial goal is unique and important. Even if you have worked on a similar goal a hundred times before, show enthusiasm about tackling his or her project. Although there are times when you will sit and listen to what the client is saying, your body language, responses, and facial expressions should portray excitement rather than disinterest and boredom. Keep eye contact with the client, smile, and show your interest in what the client is saying every time you meet or talk with him or her.

4: Keep it simple

Avoid the temptation to use financial jargon and lingo that pertains to your specialty but means nothing to your client. When you talk to your clients, address them in a style and manner that makes sense to them. Different clients like to receive information in different ways; get to know the client and respond to his or her needs. For example, some clients want to know all of the details no matter how small. Other clients only want you to tell them what they absolutely need to know and nothing more. Try to disseminate information in small increments so it is easier for the client to take in and to process.

5: Be a good listener

As a financial planner, you must listen to exactly what your client is saying. You cannot meet your client's needs unless you know what those needs are. Participate actively in a conversation with the client. Say what you need to say, but listen carefully to his or her responses.

6: Get to know your client

Find the right balance between knowing your client professionally and knowing your client on a personal level. Getting to know your client well can help you communicate better. For example, if in a discussion you learn that the client is a "morning person," you can try to schedule your meetings and phone calls with that client during times when he or she is most alert. If the client has children who play sports, occasionally ask how they are doing. Some personal situations, such as divorce or illness, directly impact a client's financial affairs. Although you may be sympathetic or deeply conscious of the client's suffering, it is important to maintain a professional distance in order to provide objective advice. At the same time, be sensitive to a client's unspoken concerns, and try to address them without directly revealing how much you know. Your job is to help your client solve his or her financial problems. A financially irresponsible spouse or a child or an indigent parent or sibling is not just the client's personal problem but also a consideration in preparing a financial plan for that family.

The Right Way to Ask Questions

Asking questions in a way that does not make you seem overbearing or intimidating is a fine art. You have to ask clients questions to uncover the details and clarify information you already have. Nothing wastes more time than working with a client only to find out later that you approached the matter incorrectly because you did not understand all of the facts. Such an incident can also cause you to lose the client. Here are some tips for client interaction:

1. Set a goal with your question

One of the first questions to ask a client is what his or her expectations are. What results is he or she trying to achieve? Once you know what the goal is, it is much easier to fill in the steps that will get your client to where he or she needs to be. Typically, this question is asked during the courting stage of the relationship, before a contact is signed, but it is a good idea to clarify that the goal is the same when you start to work together. Your understanding of the goal must match the client's understanding.

2. Lead into a question

Preface your questions by sharing information with the client. Position yourself as the expert you are by sharing knowledge and experience about the question you are about to ask. Then pose the question at the end. For example, you may use the lead-in, "Did you know that …" Sharing some information with the client in advance sets the stage for the client to give the response you need.

3. Repeat for comprehension

Once the client answers a question, restate the client's response in a follow-up question to make sure you comprehend what the client has just said. For example, if the client tells you he or she wants to accomplish three different goals, you might ask, "Can I go over the goals with you again to make sure I understand?" Then, go through the goals one at a time, and give your interpretation of what the client said.

4. Get the client to make a decision

Throughout the process of working with a client, you will reach points where the client needs to make a decision. Once the client tells you his or her choice, you still may want to confirm that the client is committed to a particular path. You can phrase the question something like, "Are you committed to …" or restate the answer for clarification. Do not repeat exactly what the client said to you like a parrot. Allow the client to hear what he or she has just said to make sure they really meant what they said.

5. Mix open-ended with close-ended questions

Ask the client the right balance of close-ended questions with "yes" or "no" answers and open-ended questions that require longer explanations. Yes-and-no questions can only get a limited amount of information from a client, but too many open-ended questions can make the client feel as though he or she is doing all of the talking. Use both types of questions to gather the information you need. Yes and no answers work well for confirmation, whereas open-ended questions encourage clients to share details, which will provide you with the information on which to base key decisions.

6. Leverage answers for new questions

Use the client's response to one question to formulate the next question. This is a good method for clarifying the client's wishes, especially after the client has given you an unexpected answer. Using the client's response in your next question helps you uncover the true intention behind that response and make sure you understand what the client wants to say.

7. Approach from a different angle

If you ask a question and do not get an appropriate response, you may have to ask the question again from a different angle. Rather than saying you do not understand the client's response, compose the question in a different way to try to get the information you need.

8. Get down to the nitty-gritty

Clients may lightly pass over a question you ask or give you a response so general that you do not know how to act upon it. Be straightforward with the client and patiently dig deeper to get the details. For example, if the client gives only a vague response when you ask what his or her goal is, ask questions to define the focus of the goal. You may even ask the client, "What do you see as our first step?"

9. Be prepared

Each meeting or discussion you have with a client should have a specific purpose. You always should conduct your own research and be prepared to accomplish the goal set for that meeting. For example, if you are helping a client develop a list of education courses to advance his or her career, research education websites for the client's industry. When you talk with the client, you will know which courses or classes to recommend and have a list of questions to help guide the client in the right direction.

Listening is just as Important as Talking

These useful suggestions can improve your listening skills:

Be an active listener

To be active, you must participate in the conversation. Although talking may not be necessary, you should react in some way to what the client is saying. Keep eye contact, shake your head, smile, or show an expression of surprise. Even though you are the listener, concentrate your full attention on the conversation.

Stay focused

It is easy for your thoughts to wander while someone is talking on and on about a subject. When you are with a client, stay focused on the client rather than thinking about what you are going to have for lunch or the other tasks you need to work on. When your thoughts are not on the conversation at hand, you are not focused. Clear your mind of everything except what the client is saying.

Take notes

Jot down notes or ask the client's permission to record your discussions. It is impossible to remember everything a client says, even when you are listening intently. Taking notes makes you a better listener because it forces you to process what you are hearing in order to get it down on paper. The speaker might not even realize what he or she is saying. Your notes will be invaluable later when you are writing up a contract or a financial plan.

Ask more questions

Responding to what a client says with a question indicates that you are listening. Asking questions and listening go hand in hand. If you listen carefully, you will be able to formulate appropriate questions, and the client will respond with useful information.

CASE STUDY: SPECIAL NEEDS OF CHILD AND ELDERLY PARENTS INSPIRE PRACTICE

Karen F. Greenberg, MBA, CFP
KF Greenberg Inc., president
Prosperity Life Planning Inc.,
director
Special Needs Tax Credit Alliance
Inc., director
kfgreenberg@cs.com
www.prosperitylifeplanning.org
www.specialneedstaxcredit.org

In the early 1980s, Karen Greenberg recalls, financial planning was becoming a "buzz word among many upwardly mobile young professional clients." As their trusted financial adviser, Greenberg was one of the first people her clients turned to as they were promoted or left jobs for new career positions, married and started families, or faced the health issues of their aging parents. The effects of inflation, high interest rates, rising real estate prices, and investments in the stock market with deductible and non-deductible IRAs moved Greenberg's clients to consult her on myriad financial issues. "I decided it would be a great idea to incorporate financial planning strategies into my practice," Greenberg says. After two years of home study through the College for Financial Planning, she became a CFP practitioner. By 1987, her home business had grown to serve 250 clients and more than a dozen small businesses.

Then, with no real warning, the unexpected happened.

After the birth of her son Ricky, who was later diagnosed with a seizure disorder and autism, Greenberg took her financial planning practice in a new direction. Recognizing that Ricky would probably have a lifetime of special needs and never be able to support himself, Greenberg faced a dilemma: How could she ensure her son would qualify for needs-based government benefits while also providing him with a good quality of life? Greenberg learned about special-needs planning, including filing for Medicaid and other public benefits, and realized many others faced the same issues she was facing with Ricky. This led Greenberg to form a nonprofit organization, Prosperity Life Planning, dedicated to educating parents with special-needs children about how to protect their own estates as well as take care of their children's needs and concerns. Through the nonprofit, Greenberg holds free workshops and consultations to provide these families with information on useful financial benefits and estate and tax information. With legal assistance, families receive the help and education they need to plan for the future with the creation of Special Needs Trusts (SNTs) and guardianship documents.

Working with parents of special-needs children has allowed Greenberg to develop a unique and important niche in her financial planning practice. Greenberg brings professional financial planning experience to her clients, but she also comes to her clients with the experience of someone who "walks in their shoes." Greenberg explores financial and life-planning strategies with her clients and sometimes incorporates life insurance, annuities, and other financial products. She offers guidance so parents can address their own retirement plans and long-term care needs while ensuring sufficient assets to take care of disabled family members.

In many areas of financial planning, it is important not only to create plans, but also to modify them as life changes. When Ricky turned 6 in 1993, Greenberg and her husband grew more concerned about the family's financial future. They revised their wills and created a Special Needs Trust for Ricky, which has enabled him to retain eligibility for such needs-based benefits as Supplemental Security Income and Medicaid. The SNT was one product of the Omnibus Budget Reconciliation Tax Act (OBRA) of 1993.

Greenberg and her husband budgeted $400 per month to fund the trust. After a year of saving and investing the funds, Greenberg wondered whether she would be able to save enough to provide for Ricky's future and looked into obtaining additional life insurance to fund the trust after she and her husband were gone. Greenberg remembered that survivorship (or second to die) life insurance covers the lives of both parents and would pay off after the second passing. At that time, the cost of a

$650,000 survivorship policy was roughly half of Greenberg's budget, $2,000 per year. The rest of the funds were invested in a diversified portfolio of mutual funds.

In addition to the SNT, they funded an education account for their daughter and contributed to each of their qualified plans for retirement. All went well until 2001, when Greenberg and her husband divorced. Greenberg was left to execute the plan alone. Fortunately, the investments in the mutual funds had grown and generated more than enough interest, dividends, and capital gains income to pay for the survivorship life insurance with tax-free dollars (because the first $3,500 of income earned by the SNT is offset by a standard deduction). Even with the downturn in the stock market that started in 2007, the combination of the mutual funds in the Special Needs Trust and the survivorship life insurance will provide at least $700,000 for Ricky's future needs, of which Greenberg and her husband contributed only $48,000 during the first 10 years. Keeping this fund as an endowment could generate $35,000 or $40,000 per year to cover his life-long expenses. Any money remaining at Ricky's passing will succeed to Greenberg's daughter and her children.

Effective Report Writing

When working with a business client, you often are required to provide formal written reports updating the client on the status of his or her financial plan. Although you may have a verbal discussion before or after (or both) you send a written report to a client, it is important that reports contain all important information, such as what stage the project has reached, any setbacks or changes, and progress made. Reports should be detailed enough to prevent misunderstandings and to give the client an accurate understanding of the project.

Clients may request updates weekly or monthly or as certain milestones are met. Your contract should include a clause specifying when and how reports will be provided. In some cases, financial advisers agree to provide reports to clients at regular intervals or only upon request from the client.

When you provide a client with a verbal report, always send the client a written follow-up. Suppose your client calls you on your cell phone for an update on his or her investment account. Tell the client what he or she wants to know, and when you return to the office, send the client an e-mail starting off with something like, "Per our conversation earlier today..." and repeating the main points of your phone conversation. Use CRM software with a cell phone or PDA to keep a record of every conversation with a client and to remind you to send follow-up e-mail or letters. Written reports reinforce clear and precise communication. The time you spend writing reports is an essential component of your working day.

Every written communication should be added to the client's files. CRM software helps you organize and keep track of these communications, so you can easily search them by date or keyword for future reference. Written records make you more efficient at writing reports. Once you have captured information in writing, you can copy and paste that text into future reports instead of having to re-create it.

Organization

The key to an effective written report is organization. Clear organization encourages the client to read a report. A disorganized report full of complex details can discourage a client and cause him or her to lay the report aside to read later. It is your responsibility as a financial planner to keep your clients informed about their affairs. Although you have technically fulfilled this responsibility by sending your client a written report, if the client does not read it, you are not accomplishing your purpose. Serious consequences could arise if a client fails to take action because he or she overlooked or ignored important information in one of your reports.

If you want to do your job well, think about your client when you are writing a report. Someone with little education, or who has difficulty understanding financial statements, will not be able to grasp the significance of a complicated report. If necessary, accompany your report with a simple summary of the most important points. When a report contains information that could affect the client's financial future or that requires action from the client, set up a meeting or phone conversation to ensure the client understands.

E-mail

E-mail is a popular and convenient way to communicate with clients, but everyone does not manage e-mail in the same way. Some people check their e-mail accounts every day, while others do not look at their e-mail for weeks. A person who receives hundreds of e-mail solicitations every week could easily overlook the e-mail containing your report. Older clients might not use e-mail at all or become confused when opening attachments. Clients may change their e-mail addresses without informing you or make a spelling mistake when they give you an e-mail address. During your initial interview with a client, ask how he or she would like to receive reports, and find out about each client's e-mail habits. If e-mail reports are a central component of your business system, your contract should contain a clause explaining when and how e-mail reports will be sent out.

After a client gives you an e-mail address during an initial interview, test the address by sending a follow-up e-mail saying something like, "It was a pleasure to meet with you today, I look forward to working with you...." If the e-mail is returned, call the client, and correct the address. Some individuals and companies have software or spam filters that block e-mail containing attachments or certain types of graphics. The first time you send out one of your reports, send a second e-mail in plain text to confirm the client has received it.

As a marketing tool, you might be sending out regular e-newsletters to people who sign up for your e-mail list. Reports and e-mail sent to individual clients should be sent from a distinct e-mail address or clearly titled in the subject line so the client does not discard them unread. Strict government regulations govern the sending of unsolicited e-mail. Your newsletters should contain a link so the recipient can unsubscribe or opt out of receiving your newsletter. Once someone has unsubscribed you can no longer send them your newsletter, but you may want to continue sending them individual reports and private messages. Avoid problems by keeping your newsletter e-mail list separate from your client e-mail directory.

Writing progress reports

Progress reports inform clients of the status of their accounts so they can ask you to make changes, if needed, to achieve the goals of their project. There is no official format for a financial planning progress report; it can be tailored to fit the needs of your client. A one-page report may be sufficient to provide all of the details.

Some clients may not be interested in receiving progress reports, while they are extremely important to others. Clarify your client's expectations at the beginning of your relationship, and include a schedule for reports in your written contract.

Always be straightforward and honest when writing a progress report. You can jeopardize your relationship with the client by trying to hide or gloss over problems. It is better to point out problems early so the client can make adjustments than to leave the client with false expectations that lead to a much greater disappointment later on,

These are the components of a typical financial planning progress report:

Overall summary

Start the report with an overall summary explaining what has been accomplished to date and letting the client know the status of his or her accounts.

Outline of accomplishments

Provide as much detail as possible about each accomplishment without being redundant. Explain what progress has been made since the previous progress report.

Completion status

Next, provide a client with a list of the completed tasks. Include the task description, date of completion, and what percentage of the overall relationship or goal has been accomplished.

Outline tasks to be completed

Outline the tasks that are pending, in order, so the client sees a picture of what you have left to do.

Issues or concerns

Describe any problems you encountered and how you did or did not overcome them. This provides the client with an opportunity to help you find a resolution.

Writing final reports

The client receives the final report when the relationship concludes. A final report signals the accomplishment of one goal, but it may be the starting point for a new goal.

The final report is similar to a progress report without a projection for the future. It should also include details and informed opinions you may have regarding the client's achievements or completion of goals. A final report is a chance to sell your services to the client for future projects. Explain what you believe is the next step. A final report includes:

Summary

The summary is a brief overview outlining the overall accomplishments made while working with the client and the goals that were not achieved.

Outline

Outline the scope of the relationship with the client and what the original goals were. You can include the methods you used to accomplish goals and what your role in guiding the client to reach the goal(s) was.

Approach

Give a detailed explanation of how you approached the project. Demonstrate to the client that you have done everything you could to successfully move the client toward goal achievement.

Recommendations

Make your recommendations and suggestions for future opportunities the client should know about now that one goal or set of goals has been reached.

Conclusion

The final portion of the report should illustrate what you accomplished and how it benefited the client.

Post-work Communication

Clients are important sources of repeat business and referrals, so even when your work with a client ends, your communication with that client should continue.

Maintain an up-to-date database of contact information for former clients so you can continue to send out information. Along with your final report, or after the final report, ask the client to fill out a survey.

Surveys gather information and feedback from the client about your services. Good reviews can be used as client testimonials to help you land new business. Poor feedback or constructive criticism can help you make adjustments to improve your financial planning business.

A client who has had a positive experience working with you can become a valuable ally. Referrals from existing clients are typically in similar circumstances and are predisposed to accept your services. Encourage current and past clients to refer new clients to you by implementing a formal referral program. Offer incentives to clients who send you referrals that turn into clients. Inform satisfied clients about your referral program as relationships end. Ask satisfied clients for testimonials to put on your website or in your marketing materials. You can also send out reminder e-mail or announcements to old clients to rekindle relationships.

CHAPTER 10

Hiring Employees and Office Support Services

As your business grows, you will need support staff to take over some of your routine duties so you can devote more time to advising clients. An office assistant can be invaluable for screening incoming calls and taking messages, producing documents, and helping file and organize client documents. A part-time bookkeeper or an accounting service can send out statements, record payments, keep track of your expenses, and help with tax preparation and filing.

You can outsource work to service companies and freelancers or hire employees to come and work in your office. Create a job description by writing down a list of job responsibilities, qualifications needed, and the number of hours per week it might take to accomplish various tasks. Decide whether you need one person to answer the phone and do multiple tasks or whether you should hire different individuals or services to handle various aspects of your business.

Friendliness, professionalism, and computer skills are key qualities to look for in a prospective employee, but you might want to specify that the candidate have a specific interest in the field of financial planning or financial services. The ideal employee could be someone looking for a mentor (a college business major, perhaps), who will be excited about getting work experience in financial planning. Such a match can be rewarding for both of you.

Ask your friends or relatives if they know anyone seeking a part-time opportunity. Place classified ads in your local paper, an online publication, or a local/national classifieds site, such as Craigslist, (**www.craigslist.org**), or Monster®, (**www.monster.com**). Write an ad describing exactly what is expected of the employee and what skills and level of experience you are seeking.

Your office helper might become a "face and voice" for your business, so choose a candidate who is personable and communicates well in person, on the phone, and in writing. Data entry and accounting or bookkeeping skills will also be useful. An added bonus would be a person who can solicit business over the phone by cold calling prospects or follow up on leads for you.

Some communities restrict the number of employees who can work in a home-based business. Check your local zoning laws and other regulations before you commit to having several people regularly park their cars in front of your house. If your HOA or zoning laws do not allow employees in a home-based business, you will be forced either to rent business space or arrange to meet your employees at job sites or other locations. Virtual employees (such as telephone answering services) or freelancers can work from their own home offices rather than on your premises.

When you begin hiring employees to help you run your financial planning business, you add a new role to your list of responsibilities — human resources manager. You must train and monitor your employees to ensure they perform their jobs properly and follow the standards and the image you have created for your business. Time sheets and payroll must be added to your accounting system. You will need to set up a personnel file for each new employee and include the appropriate forms for tax withholding. If you are not sure what is required, your accountant, your state tax officer, or your local business chamber can help. In addition to having new employees fill out tax forms, you must comply with a number of government regulations. It is important to be aware of these requirements so that you do not break the law.

Discriminatory Practices

Under Title VII, the Americans With Disabilities Act (ADA), and other legislation, it is illegal to discriminate in any aspect of employment (**www.lawmemo.com/eeoc/practices**), including:

- Hiring and firing
- Compensation, assignment, or classification of employees
- Transfer, promotion, layoff, or recall
- Job advertisements
- Recruitment
- Testing
- Use of company facilities
- Training and apprenticeship programs
- Fringe benefits

- Pay, retirement plans, and disability leave

- Other terms and conditions of employment

Discriminatory practices under these laws also include:

- Harassment based on race, color, religion, sex, national origin, disability, or age

- Retaliation against an individual for filing a charge of discrimination, participating in an investigation, or opposing discriminatory practices

- Employment decisions based on stereotypes or assumptions about the abilities, traits, or performance of individuals of a certain sex, race, age, religion, ethnic group, or individuals with disabilities

- Denying employment opportunities to a person because of marriage to, or association with, an individual of a particular race, religion, national origin, or an individual with a disability. Title VII also prohibits discrimination because of participation in schools or places of worship associated with a particular racial, ethnic, or religious group

Employers are required to post notices to all employees advising them of their rights under laws that the Equal Employment Opportunity Commission (EEOC) enforces and their right to be free from retaliation. Such notices must be accessible to persons with visual or other disabilities that affect reading.

Interviewing Candidates

The interview process begins on the telephone as you are setting a time for a personal meeting. Over the phone, you already can assess qualities such as intelligence, communication skills, friendliness, ability to inspire trust and rapport, a professional demeanor, and even a sense of humor. Remember that the person may be nervous when speaking to you for the first time. Why does a candidate want the job? Does he or she have an interest in financial planning or helping people, or does he or she just need a second job for extra income? Select several of the most suitable applicants before you schedule face-to-face meetings.

During the personal interview, apply the same standards you would expect your customers to use. How does this person present himself or herself? Is he or she well groomed, appropriately dressed for a financial services front desk, and reasonably articulate? Does he or she look you in the eye? If the prospective employee claims to have experience in the field, ask two or three questions inviting him or her to demonstrate knowledge and experience.

You do not need to act as an interrogator to uncover information about the candidate. Be friendly, funny, and make the meeting pleasant. Present a scenario and ask how the applicant would start, perform, and finish the task you describe. You want to determine to the best of your ability whether this person is being honest with you. It is acceptable to ask "what if" questions during a job interview. Discuss the job with the applicant and describe in detail what you would want that person to do. Pay attention to reactions. If the candidate responds in a way that is completely unreasonable, smile, thank him or her, and end the interview. Also, avoid applicants who present a list of demands.

252 How to Open & Operate a Financially Successful Personal Financial Planning Business

Besides friendliness, flexibility, and punctuality, attitude is important. Was the candidate more concerned about his or her own schedule or serving your needs? Was the candidate friendly or pushy and confrontational? Did he or she carry in a cup of coffee and fail to pick up the trash when leaving? How did you perceive this person's overall demeanor? Did he or she speak well of previous situations without appearing evasive or phony? Does this person seem like someone you would like to spend time with? Inexperience might not be as much of a drawback as evasiveness or dishonesty.

Do not be reluctant to hire the smartest people you can find. Ambition can work for you.

Hiring people who can be trained and promoted reassures employees that they can grow along with your company and provides incentives for superior performance.

What NOT to ask prospective employees

Antidiscrimination laws prohibit employers from asking questions about a person's religion, politics, or sexual preference during a job interview. Your questions should track the qualifications for the job, not outside interests or qualities the prospect has no control over.

Even the unintentional introduction of elements of bias and discrimination can cause problems for you. It is important to keep bias out of your interviewing and hiring process.

Make sure your employment application form does not ask for unnecessary information that might be cause for a biased or discriminatory rejection. Here are some guidelines for application forms:

- You may not ask an applicant's age. It is not appropriate or necessary. You may ask if he or she is above 18 if that is the age of majority in your state.

- You may not ask about arrest records. You may only ask about convictions and the subject of the conviction.

- You may not ask about height or weight unless these are requirements of the position. For example, some airlines have height and weight restrictions for flight attendants.

- You may not ask the applicant's country of origin, citizenship, race, parentage, or nationality. You may ask if the person is able to work in the country legally, and you may ask the person to provide proof of legal work status after hire.

- You may not ask about marital status or children.

- You may ask if the applicant has been in the military, but you may not ask about the type of discharge.

- You may not ask about the national origin of an applicant's name, but you may ask if the applicant has worked under a different name.

- You may not ask if an applicant is pregnant.

In an interview, here are some areas to avoid:

- You may not ask about children or babysitters, but you may ask if the applicant can meet the job requirements, including overtime, if it may be required.

- You may not ask about religious affiliations or organizations, but you may ask about any civic organizations or volunteer work done by the applicant.

- You may not ask if the applicant speaks other languages unless speaking another language is a specific requirement of the job.

In general, consider these two rules of thumb when interviewing and hiring applicants:

1. Everything you ask an applicant and everything you consider about an applicant should be a "bona fide occupational qualification" (BFOQ), which means it must be directly related to the job duties and qualifications you require for the position. Other questions or requirements that are not related to the job cannot be asked.

2. You can only require something of one applicant if you require it of all applicants (at least those you choose to interview), such as an intelligence test or a typing or bookkeeping test.

In your interviewing and hiring practices, avoid the appearance of bias and prejudice against an applicant. Treat all job applicants the same way and require the same things of all applicants. Avoiding questions that can be considered biased will help you avoid a possible discrimination lawsuit.

Checking references

Once you have narrowed your list down to the person or persons you want to hire, call former employers to inquire about work histories and performance. Former employers may be reluctant to offer bad news about someone, so ask specific questions.

If you just ask, "What can you tell me about Bob?" you probably will get a general answer, such as the number of years he worked for the other company or a simple, "He was all right." What you really want to know is if Bob showed up on time, did his work well, or caused any problems in the workplace. Listen for what is not being said. If the former employer has little to say, it could be a warning sign. A response such as "I would hire him again in a minute," tells you the candidate is a good employee.

Hiring a candidate

Once you have made a decision, call Bob with the good news. Let him know you have a probationary period of 60 or 90 days (longer or shorter as you choose) during which he can quit, or you can let him go with no hard feelings and no obligation on either side, depending on his performance and how he feels about the job. Send him a confirmation letter, which should be a written summary of the information provided during the interview, outlining your work policies, and what is expected of him. Putting these items into writing sets expectations and helps avoid conflicts or confusion later on.

Contact everyone else you have interviewed, and explain that you have made a decision to hire someone else. Keep the résumés of people you think might be suitable in the future. Wish everyone well, and thank them for their time.

Training and review

Set aside enough time to train your new employee(s) in the way you want the business to be run. Make your expectations clear from the first day, and put your policies in writing so there will be no misunderstandings. A written job description and employee handbook can serve as a working guide for the new employee. He or she may be spending a lot of "alone time" in the office while you are out in the field. Closely monitor the performance of the office work you assign. By clearly stating the job requirements and your expectations in the beginning, you can avoid having to retrain or fire an employee who does not do the job well.

If you have hired an office worker to take some of the administrative burden so you can spend more time with clients, you should expect to see a return on your investment in terms of increased revenue within a short period. After a few months, do a cost analysis to see if having an employee is bringing in more income or costing you more money than you expected. If hiring an office assistant has not increased your revenue as expected, consider what you can do to improve your business. For example, you could assign your employee the task of cold-calling prospective customers or managing an e-mail marketing campaign to attract more clients. You could delegate more of your routine duties to the employee so you can invest more time in marketing. Another option is to make the office assistant a part-time position. If you find that you must let the employee go, be sure to follow the guidelines specified in the hiring contract. Be careful to protect customer information and computer files in case an employee resentful at being laid off attempts to sabotage your business.

New employee paperwork

When you hire a new employee, you will have to fill out and send in or retain certain government documents. These include W-4 forms, the Employee's Withholding Allowance Certificate, and the W-5 for employees with a child if they qualify for advance payment of earned income credit. Go to the IRS site (**www.irs.gov**) to download forms and for more specific information. You also are required to report newly hired employees to your state. The Small Business Administration website (**www.sba.gov/content/new-hire-reporting-your-state**) links to information about each state.

WHAT TO INCLUDE IN THE EMPLOYEE FILE

After you have hired a candidate, immediately create an individual employee file that contains the following information:

❑ A W-4

❑ Current and previous performance evaluations

❑ Date employment commenced

❑ Emergency phone number(s) for the employee

❑ Job title

❑ Rate of pay

❑ Signed and dated statement acknowledging that the employee has read and accepts the terms of the employee handbook/policy manual

❑ Termination date, if the employee leaves, and a detailed reason for why the employee has been terminated

❑ The employee's application

❑ The employee's legal name, address, and phone number

❑ The employee's Social Security number

Application of federal law to employers

A number of factors may cause an employer to be covered by a federal employment law. These include the number of individuals employed by a business; whether an employer is a private entity or a branch of federal, state, or local government; and the type of industry in which an employer is involved.

The following chart shows how the number of workers a company employs determines if a specific federal statute applies to the business.

Number of Employees	Applicable Statute
100	WARN — Worker Adjustment and Retraining Notification Act
50	FMLA — Family Medical Leave Act
20	ADEA — Age Discrimination in Employment Act
20	COBRA — Consolidated Omnibus Benefits Reconciliation Act
20	OWBPA — Older Workers Benefit Protection Act
15	ADA — Americans with Disabilities Act
15	GINA — Genetic Information Nondiscrimination Act
15	Title VII of the Civil Rights Act of 1964
15	PDA — Pregnancy Discrimination Act
1	EPPA — Employee Polygraph Protection Act
1	EPA — Equal Pay Act
1	FRCA — Fair Credit Reporting Act
1	FLSA — Fair Labor Standards Act
1	IRCA — Immigration Reform and Control Act
1	OSHA — Occupational Safety and Health Act
1	PRWORA — Personal Responsibility and Work Opportunity Reconciliation Act
1	USERRA — Uniform Services Employment and Reemployment Rights Act

Outsourcing

By using a third-party service or a freelancer to do some of your administrative work, you can get help without the added expense of salaries, benefits, and providing office space with a desk, computer, and phone line. Typically, you are only responsible for paying them for the work they complete for you.

Third-party services such as virtual offices, accounting services, and attorneys typically charge a flat monthly fee or an hourly fee. They usually can provide you with a rate schedule, a description of their services, and a list of references.

Finding freelancers can be as much work as hiring employees because you have to find qualified candidates, conduct interviews, and try out different individuals until you find someone who is a good fit. Once you have located the right person, though, your working relationship can be fruitful. A freelancer often brings expertise and experience to the job and is familiar with the technologies and processes used by similar businesses.

Because you probably will need to meet regularly with your freelancers, start by looking for someone in your own neighborhood. Ask for recommendations from friends, family members, and local business owners. Post job listings in the career centers at local colleges and universities and with local job services Contact local chapters of professional associations. You can post freelance jobs on career and job websites such as Monster (**www.monster.com**), CareerBuilder® (**www.careerbuilder.com**), Sologig.com (**www.sologig.com**), IFreelance. com (**www.ifreelance.com**), Freelancer.com (**www.freelancer.com**) and Yahoo!® HotJobs (**http://hotjobs.yahoo.com**) for a fee. You can also use free classified websites such as Craigslist (**www.craigslist.com**), Kijiji (**www.ebayclassifieds.com**), and Backpage.com® (**www.backpage.com**). IFreelance.com, Freelancer.com, and Elance® (**www.elance.com**) broker freelance services online and take a commission from the payment for each job.

Conclusion

A personal financial planning business is based almost entirely on you — your education, your skills, your personality, and your interests. Clients come to you because they trust you to help them with an important aspect of their lives — their financial security. Working with them can be fulfilling, both personally and financially. Every independent financial planner eventually develops a niche or a specialty catering to a particular type of client, community, or service.

You will not be ready to start your own financial planning business until you are confident you have the skills and experience to give your clients the best service. One success leads to another. A client who believes you have done an excellent job will recommend you to others. When you have a reputation for doing exceptional work, people will be willing to pay more for your services. If you do not feel prepared to start out on your own yet, spend some time working for someone else and learning the business. As you have learned from this book, you cannot expect to make a living right away as a personal financial planner. Working at a job in the financial services industry, or for an established financial planner, will give you time to gather your resources and make useful contacts with whom you can network in the future.

It is a big step from doing financial analysis or managing investments to running your own business. Financial acumen is only one of the qualities of a successful personal financial planner. You must also be able to win and maintain the confidence of many types of people, to be perceptive to their needs, and to handle their emotions in delicate situations. The professional relationship between a financial planner and a client can last for months and years, during which both the economy and the client's personal life can go through many ups and downs. An experienced mentor can be invaluable in teaching you how to navigate your relationships with your clients successfully.

In addition to developing interpersonal skills, you also have to manage your own finances and ensure your business is making enough income to support itself and be worth your while. You are responsible for many duties which your previous employers took care of in the past: keeping accounts, collecting payments, filing taxes, hiring and paying employees, organizing files and documents, and marketing. Time management is essential so you can keep up with all these tasks and still have time to devote to your clients. You may feel overwhelmed at first until you establish a routine and a work schedule. I hope this book will help you with many of your new responsibilities.

Starting your own business is exciting. You will be challenged as you encounter unexpected obstacles, make mistakes, and discover what you do best. There is no doubt that three or four years from now, you will know a great deal more than you know today. Do not allow small disruptions to distract you from your goal. Keep going, and you will be rewarded with the personal satisfaction of serving those who need you most while doing what you enjoy.

What is Your Preference?

If you have turned to this section, you may be ready to take stock of your career preferences. Here are a few questions to ponder:

- Do you hate to be told what to do?

- Are you motivated or a couch potato?

- How do you react to the joke, "Yeah, I make my own schedule. I get to decide which 80 hours of the week I work." What does that reaction indicate to you?

- Are you a born delegator, or are you more "hands-on?" *Can* you delegate, or are you bent on doing everything yourself?

If you have effectively thought all of this through, you may not need to spend time with the following checklist. But if you have not really considered some of these factors, do it now. *You* are the core of your potential new business, and you will need to know what makes *you* tick.

Personality Quiz

1.	I am happiest when I am completely in charge of a project and using my own ideas.	Yes	No	Sometimes
2.	I prefer to have a group of people brainstorm alternatives and then come to a group consensus to set priorities and make decisions.	Yes	No	Sometimes
3.	I like to have someone else with more experience set my targets and goals so I can meet or exceed them.	Yes	No	Sometimes
4.	I am excited about starting from scratch.	Yes	No	Sometimes
5.	I enjoy building teams as long as I am the leader.	Yes	No	Sometimes
6.	I feel uptight if someone asks me a question, and I do not immediately know the answer.	Yes	No	Sometimes
7.	I enjoy pleasing the people I work for.	Yes	No	Sometimes
8.	I want to help my employees feel successful, and I know how to encourage others.	Yes	No	Sometimes
9.	My primary goal is to make a lot of money fast and have lots of leisure time.	Yes	No	Sometimes
10.	I like the idea of coming to work later in the morning and seeing my employees already working.	Yes	No	Sometimes
11.	I know I do not know how to do everything, but I am willing to ask for advice and even pay for it.	Yes	No	Sometimes
12.	I would rather learn on the job by trial and error than pay for help.	Yes	No	Sometimes

13.	I would rather sit in my office making phone calls and setting appointments than working outside getting sweaty.	Yes	No	Sometimes
14.	I do not care if I have to follow someone else's rules if I benefit from his or her expertise and make more money faster.	Yes	No	Sometimes
15.	I work outdoors, and I play outdoors. It is my favorite place to be.	Yes	No	Sometimes
16.	I hate being cooped up in an office.	Yes	No	Sometimes
17.	I have excellent mechanical skills.	Yes	No	N/A
18.	I know I am good at what I do, but I know my limits.	Yes	No	Sometimes
19.	I am orderly by nature. I live by the motto: "a place for everything and everything in its place."	Yes	No	Sometimes
20.	Even if my work area seems messy, it is organized to suit my needs.	Yes	No	Sometimes
21.	I like the challenge of getting along with difficult people.	Yes	No	Sometimes
22.	One of my goals is to inspire others to succeed. I want to be a role model in my community.	Yes	No	Sometimes
23.	I would like a job where I can get my hands dirty.	Yes	No	Sometimes
24.	I prefer the wilderness to a manicured golf course.	Yes	No	Sometimes
25.	I keep my checkbook balanced and promptly reconcile bank statements.	Yes	No	Sometimes
26.	I pay my taxes on time.	Yes	No	Sometimes
27.	I know the local regulations for the business I want to open.	Yes	No	N/A

		Yes	No	Sometimes
28.	I feel comfortable negotiating prices with customers and vendors.	Yes	No	Sometimes
29.	I like to associate with people from different backgrounds.	Yes	No	Sometimes
30.	I will tell an employee the result I want and let him or her figure out how to achieve it.	Yes	No	Sometimes
31.	I am rarely satisfied, and I always strive for improvement.	Yes	No	Sometimes
32.	I have always enjoyed working with numbers.	Yes	No	N/A
33.	I am willing to change any business practice or product at a moment's notice if I hear of something that might work better.	Yes	No	Sometimes
34.	I hate having someone else tell me what to do or how to do it.	Yes	No	Sometimes
35.	I am done with formal education forever.	Yes	No	Maybe
36.	I will ask customers for feedback regularly. If I do not hear complaints, I will not change anything in the business.	Yes	No	Sometimes
37.	I like to shop for bargains.	Yes	No	Sometimes
38.	I do not take chances; I plan for all possibilities.	Yes	No	Sometimes
39.	I can be fine without a regular paycheck for a while.	Yes	No	Sometimes
40.	I am eager to open this business. It is like a parachute jump — a leap into the unknown.	Yes	No	Sometimes

41.	I have enough of my own money and resources to start this business immediately.	Yes	No	Sometimes
42.	I know where to get more money if I need it.	Yes	No	Sometimes
43.	I am living from paycheck to paycheck now. I am tired of it.	Yes	No	Sometimes
44.	I want customers ready and waiting the day I open my doors.	Yes	No	Sometimes
45.	I have many ideas about marketing my business, and I know how to get it done.	Yes	No	Sometimes
46.	I already have a company name picked out.	Yes	No	N/A
47.	I already know what kind of customers I want to serve.	Yes	No	N/A
48.	I dream about this business at night.	Yes	No	Sometimes
49.	I have a picture in my head of me running my own business.	Yes	No	Sometimes
50.	My family and friends are supportive of my business ideas.	Yes	No	Sometimes

Scoring:

If you answered "yes" on questions **1, 4, 5, 8, 12, 33, 34, 39, 41, 42, 48, 49,** and **50,** business ownership might be for you. These responses show you have an independent spirit and are willing to take full responsibility for the job you are undertaking.

If you answered "yes" on question **2**, you might want to form a partnership or at least consider bringing employees, family, or other advisers to help you make business decisions.

If you answered "yes" on questions **3**, **14**, and **50**, you might want to consider franchise ownership.

If you answered "yes" to **41**, **42**, and **44**, you may find purchasing an existing business more appropriate than starting from scratch.

If you answered "yes" to questions **18** and **30**, you probably have significant delegating skills.

If you answered "yes" to questions **11**, **21**, **22**, **38**, and **40**, you have a good attitude that will be helpful in business.

If you answered "yes" to **15**, **16**, **17**, **19**, **20**, **23**, **25**, **26**, **27**, **28**, **29**, **31**, **32**, **37**, **45**, **46**, and **47**, you have many of the skills and affinities useful to business operation.

Finally, if you answered "yes" to questions **9**, **10**, **13**, **24**, **35**, **36**, and **43**, you might find the reality of business ownership difficult. This does *not* mean you cannot run a successful business, just as a "no" to certain questions in the skills and affinities group does not mean you cannot succeed. But, it *does* mean you may need to select partners who have complementary talents or get some training yourself. It is always a good idea to consider delegating tasks that do not suit your skill set. Also, remember that showing your employees you are dedicated to the job will inspire them to give their best efforts, too.

Sample Articles of Organization

Articles of Organization for an LLC filed in the state of Florida will look something like this:

ARTICLE I — Name

The name and purpose of the Limited Liability Company is:

Fictitious Name International Trading Company, LLC
Purpose: To conduct…

ARTICLE II — Address

The mailing address and street address of the principal office of the Limited Liability Company is:

Street Address: 1234 International Trade Drive
Beautiful City, FL 33003

Mailing Address: P.O. Box 1235

Beautiful City, FL 33003

ARTICLE III — Registered Agent, Registered Office, and Registered Agent's Signature

The name and the Florida street address of the registered agent are:

John Doe

5678 New Company Lane

Beautiful City, FL 33003

Having been named as registered agent and to accept service of process for the above stated Limited Liability Company at the place designated in this certificate, I hereby accept the appointment as registered agent and agree to act in this capacity. I further agree to comply with the provisions of all statutes relating to the proper and complete performance of my duties, and I am familiar with and accept the obligations of my position as a registered agent as provided for in Chapter 608, Florida Statutes.

_____

Registered Agent's Signature

ARTICLE IV — Manager(s) or Managing Member(s)

Title   **Name & Address**

"MGR" = Manager

"MGRM" = Managing Member

MGR   Jane Doe
                             234 Manager Street
                             Beautiful City, FL 33003

MGRM   Jim Unknown
                             789 Managing Member Drive
                             Beautiful City, FL 33003

ARTICLE V — Effective Date

The effective date of this Florida Limited Liability Company shall be January 1, 2009.

REQUIRED SIGNATURE:

_____

Signature of a member or an authorized representative of a member

Where to File Articles of Incorporation

Finding appropriate state offices can be a challenge. Offices serving similar functions may go by different names. Here is a shortcut so you can reach the appropriate office for filing Articles of Incorporation without having to search through the maze of governmental agencies in your state:

State	Secretary of State's Office (specific division within)
Alabama	Corporations Division
Alaska	Corporations, Businesses, and Professional Licensing
Arizona	Corporation Commission
Arkansas	Business / Commercial Services
California	Business Portal
Colorado	Business Center
Connecticut	Commercial Recording Division
Delaware	Division of Corporations
Florida	Division of Corporations
Georgia	Corporations Division
Hawaii	Business Registration Division
Idaho	Business Entities Division
Illinois	Business Services Department
Indiana	Corporations Division
Iowa	Business Services Division
Kansas	Business Entities
Kentucky	Corporations
Louisiana	Corporations Section
Maine	Division of Corporations
Maryland	Secretary of State
Massachusetts	Corporations Division
Michigan	Business Portal
Minnesota	Business Services
Mississippi	Business Services
Missouri	Business Portal
Montana	Business Services

State	Secretary of State's Office (specific division within)
Nebraska	Business Services
Nevada	Commercial Recordings Division
New Hampshire	Corporation Division
New Jersey	Business Formation and Registration
New Mexico	Corporations Bureau
New York	Division of Corporations
North Carolina	Corporate Filings
North Dakota	Business registrations
Ohio	Business Services
Oklahoma	Business Filing Department
Oregon	Corporation Division
Pennsylvania	Corporation Bureau
Rhode Island	Corporations Division
South Carolina	Business Filings
South Dakota	Corporations
Tennessee	Division of Business Services
Texas	Corporations Section
Utah	Division of Corporations and Commercial Code
Vermont	Corporations
Virginia	Business Information Center
West Virginia	Business Organizations
Washington	Corporations
Washington, DC	Corporations Division
Wisconsin	Corporations
Wyoming	Corporations Division

Insurance Checklist

Type of Insurance	Mandatory?	Coverage/$	Cost/$
Comprehensive liability	Yes / No		
Product liability	Yes / No		
Workers' compensation	Yes / No		
Home-based business	Yes / No		
Key person	Yes / No		
Criminal	Yes / No		
Business interruption	Yes / No		
Vehicle(s)	Yes / No		
		Total Insurance Cost	$

Other insurance options/needs:

_____

_____

_____

_____

Sample Client Intake Forms

Financial Profile

Data Gathering Checklist and Receipt

Most recent financial statements and records concerning your:

- ❑ Last paycheck stub(s)
- ❑ Loan statements and credit card statements
- ❑ Mortgage statements (last statement)
- ❑ Investment statements (last statement)
- ❑ Retirement programs (last statement)
- ❑ Most recent federal and state income tax returns
- ❑ Insurance policies (original policy, recent statement, dec pages)
    - ❑ Life
    - ❑ Disability

      ❑ Long term care

      ❑ Home and auto

      ❑ Umbrella liability

❑ Employee benefit statements or booklet

❑ Checking and money market accounts (last 2 statements)

❑ Business or partnership agreements

❑ Wills and trust agreements

❑ Other pertinent financial data _____

❑ Other pertinent financial data _____

All information provided will be held in the strictest confidence.

I understand these documents will be used in the preparation of my written Financial Plan and authorize their use.

_____   _____

CLIENT   DATE

I accept receipt of the above listed documents.

_____   _____

FINANCIAL PLANNER   DATE

Sample Financial Planning Agreement

This Financial Services Agreement ("Agreement") is entered into by and between a Registered Investment Adviser (RIA) and _____ Investment Adviser Representative ("IAR") and _____ ("Client"), whereby Client desires to receive financial planning services as outlined below.

1. FINANCIAL PLANNING SERVICES AND FEES

Provide personal financial planning services that are consistent with the client's objectives and goals. The financial plan may include retirement planning, educational planning, estate planning, major purchase planning, business succession planning, and insurance needs and analysis. Legal and tax advice will not be provided.

The client will be charged on a flat rate ranging from $0 to $20,000, depending on the complexity of the financial situation, or an hourly rate of no more than $300 per hour. Fees will be disclosed before the Financial Planning Agreement is signed, and in the case of an hourly fee, the client will be provided an estimate of the number of hours it requires to provide this service.

Half of the estimated fee will be paid upon the signing of the Agreement, and the second half of the fee will be paid upon completion and delivery of the financial plan or report to the client.

2. POTENTIAL CONFLICTS OF INTEREST

The IAR is a registered representative with XX Financial (XX), a licensed insurance agent through numerous insurance companies, and an Investment Adviser Representative with XX.

IAR may suggest that clients implement recommendations set forth in the financial plan and consulting services through XX in his capacity as a registered representative with XX or an independent licensed insurance agent. If the client chooses to do so, this would present a conflict of interest to the extent that IAR would receive normal and customary commissions as a registered representative or licensed insurance agent resulting from any securities or insurance transactions.

The financial planning services may include generic recommendations as to general types of investment products, securities, or insurance that may be appropriate for the Client to purchase given his/her financial situation and objectives. The Client is under no obligation to purchase such securities or insurance through XX and the IAR.

3. CONFIDENTIALITY

None of the information and data that Client provides to RIA and IAR will be disclosed by RIA and IAR to any other non-related firm, person, or entity without prior consent of Client, unless such disclosure is required by law. Client acknowledges, understands, and agrees that for our mutual protection, RIA may electronically record telephone conversations. Client agrees not to record any telephone conversation without the express written authorization of RIA and the individual(s) engaged in the conversation.

4. ASSIGNMENT/TERMINATION

This Agreement may not be assigned or transferred in any manner by any party without the written consent of all parties receiving or rendering services hereunder. This Agreement may be terminated by any party effective upon receipt of written notice to the other parties ("Termination Date"). Client will be entitled to a refund of unearned fees, if any, based upon the time and effort completed before termination of the Agreement. The Agreement is terminated upon final consultation with the client. No refunds will be made after delivery of the consulting services, except when the number of actual hours is fewer than the estimated number of hours quoted. Termination of the Agreement will not affect the liabilities or obligations of the parties for activity initiated before termination.

5. PRACTICE OF LAW AND ACCOUNTING

RIA is not licensed to engage in the practice of law or accounting and, consequently, will offer no legal or accounting advice when consulting with Client. None of the fee for services under this Agreement relate to accounting or legal services. If such services are necessary, it shall be the responsibility of the Client to obtain them.

6. SEVERABILITY

If any provision of this Agreement shall be held or made nonenforceable by a statute, rule, regulation, decision of a tribunal or otherwise, such provision shall be automatically reformed and construed, so as to be valid, operative, and enforceable to the maximum extent permitted by law or equity while most nearly preserving its original intent. The invalidity of any part of this Agreement shall not render invalid the remainder of this Agreement and, to that extent, the provision of this Agreement shall be deemed severable.

7. GOVERNING LAW

This Agreement shall be construed under the laws of the State.

8. ARBITRATION

Client agrees to direct any complaints regarding the handling of Client's plan to IAR in writing. Any dispute involving Client relating to this Agreement that cannot be settled shall be taken to arbitration as set forth below:

- Arbitration is final and binding on the parties.
- The parties waive their right to seek remedies in court, including the right to a jury trial.
- Pre-arbitration discovery is generally more limited than and different from court proceedings.

- The arbitrators' award is not required to include factual findings or legal reason, and any party's right to appeal or to seek modification of rulings by the arbitrators is strictly limited.

- The panel of arbitrators will typically include a minority of arbitrators who were or are affiliated with the securities industry.

Any controversy between RIA, IAR, and Client arising out of our business or this Agreement shall be submitted to arbitration conducted before the American Arbitration Association in accordance with their rules. Arbitration must be commenced by service upon the other parties of a written demand for arbitration or a written notice of intention to arbitrate. The party seeking arbitration will elect the arbitrating tribunal. No person shall bring a putative certified class action to arbitration nor seek to enforce any pre-dispute arbitration agreement against any person who has initiated in a court a putative class action or who is a member of a putative class action who has not opted out of the class with respect to any claims encompassed by the putative class action until; (i) the class certification is denied, or (ii) the class is decertified, or (iii) the client is excluded from the class by the court. Such forbearance to enforce an agreement to arbitrate shall not constitute a waiver of any rights under this Agreement except to the extent stated herein.

9. RECEIPT OF CMA'S FORM ADV PART II

Client acknowledges receipt of RIA's Form ADV Part II. Unless Client received said Form ADV Part II at least forty-eight (48) hours before execution of this Agreement, Client may cancel this Agreement within five (5) days of execution by giving written notice of such cancellation to IAR. This Agreement will not take effect until at least forty-eight (48) hours after Client has received RIA's Form ADV Part II and RIA has accepted this agreement.

10. FINANCIAL SERVICES PROFILE

The Financial Services Profile, (below) incorporated herein by reference and made a part of this Agreement, must be completed in full by Client, where applicable, and the Client hereby acknowledges the accuracy of its contents.

Financial Planning Profile

Instructions: Complete all sections of this profile with the assistance of your investment adviser representative (IAR).

1. Client name	**Social Security/tax ID number**
Client address	**Phone number**

2. Investment adviser representative name   **Phone number**

3. Type of plan (select one)
- ○ Initial plan
- ○ Progress report
  (for annual review)

4. Financial planning fee (select one)
- ○ Fixed fee amount:
  $
- ○ Hourly fee

Hourly rate: $
Estimated hours: ×
Estimated total fee: $

5. Type of payment   ○ Initial   ○ Final
Payment Method (select one)
- ○ Check attached
- ○ Defer portion of payment until receipt of written
  financial plan

6. Investment objective
Please choose the investment objective that most
accurately reflects your current overall goals.
- ○ *Income with capital preservation.* Emphasis
  is placed on generation of current income and
  prevention of capital loss.
- ○ *Income with moderate growth.* Emphasis is placed
  on generation of current income with a secondary
  focus on moderate capital growth.
- ○ *Growth with income.* Emphasis is placed on modest
  capital growth with some focus on generation of
  current income.
- ○ *Growth.* Emphasis is placed on achieving high long-
  term growth and capital appreciation. There is little
  focus on generation of current income.
- ○ *Aggressive growth.* Emphasis is placed on
  aggressive growth and maximum capital
  appreciation. There is no focus on generation of
  current income.

**7. Please check those areas of analysis that you would
like to have included in your financial plan.** (Select all
that apply.)
- ○ Retirement planning
- ○ Disability insurance planning
- ○ Education planning
- ○ Long term care needs
- ○ Life insurance needs
- ○ Estate planning needs
- ○ Major purchase planning

8. Client acknowledgement and execution:
This Financial Planning Agreement contains a pre-dispute clause in section 8, which begins on page 3. Client
acknowledges receiving a copy of this Agreement and Financial Planning Profile, and of Form ADV Part 2.

Agreement and Financial Profile agreed to on: M M / D D / Y Y Y Y

Client signature	Client name (print)	Date
Client signature	Client name (print)	Date
Investment adviser representative signature	Investment adviser representative name (print)	Date

11. ENTIRE AGREEMENT

This Agreement represents the entire agreement between the parties with respect to the subject matter contained herein. The Agreement may be amended upon thirty (30) days notice to all parties.

12. NOTICES

All written notices to any party under this Agreement shall be sent to such party by first class mail, facsimile transmission, or e-mail at the address set forth or such other address as such party may designate in writing to the other.

I _____ (Client) acknowledge that I have received RIA's ADV Form Part II, Schedule F, Financial Planning Agreement, and Privacy Policy (follows this page) on _____ (date).
                                                              MM / DD / YYYY

_____   _____   _____
(Client signature)   (Client name printed)   (Date)

_____   _____   _____
(Client signature)   (Client name printed)   (Date)

_____   _____   _____
(Adviser signature)   (Adviser name printed)   (Date)

_____   _____   _____
(Adviser signature)   (Adviser name printed)   (Date)

Sample Client Questionnaire

Personal Information

	Client 1	Client 2
First name, MI		
Last name		
Sex		
Birth date	/ /	/ /
Age at retirement		
Inflation: assumed %		
E-mail address		
Social Security #	- -	- -
Address		
City		

	Client 1	Client 2
State/ZIP		
Phone		
Position		
Employer		
Address		
City		
State/ZIP		
Phone		

Children's names	Birth date	4-year college?

Financial Goals

Rank the following priorities from 1 being the highest priority to 7 the lowest. ***Do not*** *use the same number twice.* **SKIP any that do not apply.**

Priorities	Rank (1-7)
Achieve financial security for retirement.	
Provide funds for education.	
Achieve other goals. (List them:)	
Maintain adequate life insurance.	
Protect your resources in case of disability.	
Maximize the potential return on investments given your risk profile.	
Reduce estate taxes and provide for your heirs.	

Risk Tolerance

The various investment vehicles available today are characterized by different levels of risk and potential return. Complete this section to assess your level of risk tolerance.

1. Over the next five years, do you expect your financial situation to:

A.   Dramatically improve

B.   Improve somewhat

C.   Stay about the same

D.   Worsen

2. Select the asset allocation service most useful to you. For most investors, an objective recommendation that considers your entire investor profile (time horizon, risk tolerance, etc.) is the most appropriate service. However, some investors prefer to ignore many elements of their investor profile and target a narrow range of returns. Also, some investors may wish to limit their investments to either all stock or all bond investments. Please indicate below which of these options appeals to you.

A.   I wish to receive an objective evaluation that considers my entire profile.

B.   I wish to target a narrow range of returns while trying to minimize risk.

C.   I have considered my other investments and wish to limit my investments to *stock portfolios*.

D.   I have considered my other investments and wish to limit my investments to *bond portfolios*.

3. When Investing, there is a natural trade-off between investment performance and the risk of a decline in portfolio value. Typically, the higher the return you pursue, the more willing you must be to suffer losses. Please review the following hypothetical investment choices and their risk and return characteristics. Select the investment that would be most likely to meet your expectations for returns in "average" or "good" years without making you uncomfortable during periods of declining values. Past performance is not indicative of future results.

		Potential return in a bad year	Potential return in an average year	Potential return in a good year
A.	Investment A	-1%	+6	+10
B.	Investment B	-4%	+8	+16
C.	Investment C	-8%	+10	+24
D.	Investment D	-11%	+12	+30
E.	Investment E	-16%	+14	+35

4. Over an investment cycle of 5 to 7 years, some investments experience different returns from year to year. The table below shows the annual change in value of four hypothetical $100,000 portfolios. Please keep in mind that past performance is no guarantee of future results. Please select the investment with the five-year return best suited for your goals and tolerance for short-term losses in a given year:

		Year 1	Year 2	Year 3	Year 4	Year 5	Annualized average return
A.	Portfolio "A"	-14,000	31,800	30,600	-6,700	42,500	13.0%
B.	Portfolio "B"	-10,000	27,000	22,100	-4,200	33,700	11.0%
C.	Portfolio "C"	-6,000	18,800	17,900	-1,300	24,600	9.0%
D.	Portfolio "D"	-2,000	8,800	12,800	3,600	17,200	7.0%

5. The graph below shows the returns of a hypothetical investment over time. If you owned this investment, given its historical and current returns, what action could you take (Past performance is not indicative of future results):

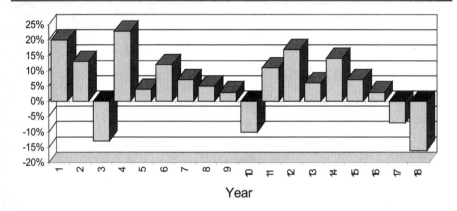

Year

A.	I would immediately sell all of the investment and cut my losses.
B.	I would sell some of the investment to protect myself from further loss.
C.	I would continue to hold the investment with the expectation of higher future returns.
D.	I would invest more now since the price is lower.

6. Which statement most accurately describes you as an investor?

A.	Aggressive	D.	Moderately conservative
B.	Moderately Aggressive	E.	Conservative
C.	Moderate		

Sample Expense Sheet

	Monthly	Annual*
INCOME (Part A)		
Employment Income		
Salary/wages		
Self employment (actual)		
Self employment (taxable)		
Other Income		
Taxable pensions		
Social Security benefits		
Other taxable		
Other non-taxable		
TOTAL — Part A		
TAXES (Part B)		
Federal income taxes		
State/local income taxes		

*or indicate other mode of payment

	Monthly	*Annual**
Property taxes		
Medicare/Social Security		
Other		
TOTAL — Part B		

BASIC EXPENSES (Part C)

Housing		
Rent		
Gas/oil		
Electric		
Telephone / cellular		
Water / sewer		
HOA dues		
Maintenance		
Cable / satellite TV		
Lawn and pool		
Major improvements		
Transportation		
Lease payment		
Maintenance and repairs		
Gas		
Commuting fees / tolls		
Food		
Groceries		
Lunches		
Clothing		
Basic apparel		

	Monthly	*Annual**
Uniforms / children clothes		
Dry cleaning / laundering		
Medical / dental expenses		
Co-payments / deductibles		
Dental / orthodontics		
Prescriptions		
Other basic expenses		
Grooming / salon		
Child care		
Pet care		
School supplies		
Alimony / child support		
Insurance		
Automobile		
Homeowners		
Life		
Disability income		
Health		
Umbrella		
Boat		
TOTAL — Part C		
DISCRETIONARY LIFESTYLE (Part D)		
Charitable contributions		
Gifts		
Entertainment / dining		
Recreation / travel		

	Monthly	*Annual**
Club dues		
Hobbies		
Other		
Funding for long-term objectives		
College education		
Client — retirement plans		
Spouse — retirement rlans		
Other retirement (IRAs)		
Other		
Short-term objectives		
Emergency fund		
Vacations		
Special occasions (weddings, bat mitsva, etc.)		
Gifting programs		
TOTAL — Part D		

CURRENT OBLIGATIONS (Part E)

Short-term obligations	Creditor	Amount	Interest rate	Current monthly payment	Owner
Consumer credit	VISA				
	MasterCard				
	AMEX				
	Discover				
	Other				
Installment loans					
Personal loans					

Long-term obligations					
Mortgage 1					
Mortgage 2					
Home equity					
Vehicle 1					
Vehicle 2					
Investment loans					
Business loans					
Other obligations					
TOTAL — Part E					

	INCOME	TOTAL Part A
minus	**EXPENSES**	TOTAL Part B
		TOTAL Part C
		TOTAL Part D
		TOTAL Part E

equals	**EXCESS DISCRETIONARY INCOME**

Excess discretionary income willing to save

Notes:

_____

_____

_____

_____

_____

_____

Income and Expense Worksheet Instructions

Use this form to record annual cash income and expenditures for the last year. We use this information in combination with your expenditures to analyze current spending patterns.

When totaling **Parts A through E**, remember to multiply monthly payments by 12.

Employment income (Part A)

Salary/wages

Enter your total gross taxable wages and salaries. Include the amount of any salary reduction contributions in this amount (i.e., DO NOT reduce the total by any contributions).

Self-employment (actual cash)

Enter the actual money received from self-employment.

Self-employment (taxable amount)

Enter the amount as shown on IRS Form 1040, schedule C as Business Income. This amount could be the same as *Self-employment (actual cash)*.

Other income

Taxable pensions

Enter the fully taxable pensions and taxable portions of other pensions.

Social Security

Enter the total annual Social Security benefits received.

Other taxable income

Enter other taxable income such as lottery winnings and other gains (IRS Form 4797).

Other non-taxable income

Enter other non-taxable income. Include the portions of pensions not subject to tax. Do not enter any non-taxable interest or dividends here.

Taxes (Part B)

Enter amounts as shown on IRS Form 1040 or schedule C.

Basic expenses (Part C)

Housing

Enter costs of items listed as well as any additional items associated with running the residence.

Transportation

Enter costs of items listed as well as any additional items associated with transportation needs.

Food

Enter food costs. Do not forget lunches and dining out.

Clothing

Self explanatory

Medical/dental expenses

Enter medical expenses that have not been reimbursed.

Other basic expenses

Enter items listed and/or additional basic expenses.

Insurance

Enter all payments towards insurance coverage(s).

Discretionary lifestyle (Part D)

Enter items listed and/or additional discretionary expenses.

Funding for long-term objectives

Enter the amount that you are currently setting aside each year for objectives listed and/or additional long-term objectives.

Short-term objectives

Enter the amount you are currently setting aside this year for objectives listed and/or additional short-term objectives.

Short-term obligations

Enter all payments towards short-term obligations.

Long-term obligations

Enter all payments towards long-term obligations.

Current obligations (Part E)

These are your debts and loans. Include any money you owe to creditors. Please include the amount owed, the interest rate on the debt, and the amount of the monthly payment, and whose obligation it is.

APPENDIX H

Sample Adviser Registration

FORM ADV

Uniform Application for Investment Adviser Registration

Name of investment adviser:	
Address: *(number and street)* *(city)* *(state)* *(zip)*	Area code: telephone number:

This part of FORM ADV gives information about the investment adviser and his or her business for the use of clients.

The information has not been approved or verified by any government authority.

Table of Contents

(Schedule A, B, C, D, and E are included with Part I of this Form for
the use of regulatory bodies and are not distributed to clients.)

Potential persons who are to respond to the collection of information
contained in this form are not required to respond unless the form displays a
currently valid OMB control number.

*Answer all items. Complete amended pages in full, circle amended
items, and file with execution page (page 1)*

FORM ADV

Applicant:	SEC File Number: 801-	Date:

1. A. Advisory services and fees. *(Check the applicable boxes.)*
For each type of service provided, state the approximate % of total
advisory billings from that service. *(See instruction below.)*

Applicant:

❏ (1)   Provides investment supervisory services.............. _____%

❑ (2) Manages investment advisory accounts not involving investment supervisory services.............. _____%

❑ (3) Furnishes investment advice through consultations not included in either service described above...................................... _____%

❑ (4) Issues periodicals about securities by subscription.. _____%

❑ (5) Issues special reports about securities not included in any service described above .... _____%

❑ (6) Issues, not as part of any service described above, any charts, graphs, formulas, or other devices that clients may use to evaluate securities _____

❑ (7) On more than an occasional basis, furnishes advice to clients on matters not involving securities .... _____%

❑ (8) Provides a timing service .... %

❑ (9) Furnishes advice about securities in any manner not described above .... _____

(Percentages should be based on applicant's last fiscal year. If applicant has not completed its first fiscal year, provide estimates of advisory billings for that year and state that the percentages are estimates.)

B. Does applicant call any of the services it checked above financial planning or some similar term? .... ❑ Yes ❑ No

---

C. Applicant offers investment advisory services for: *(check all that apply)*

❑ (1) A percentage of assets under management

❑ (2) Hourly charges

❑ (3) Fixed fees (not including subscription fees)

❑ (4) Subscription fees

❑ (5) Commissions

❑ (6) Other

D. For each checked box in A above, describe on Schedule F:

- The services provided, including the name of any publication or report issued by the adviser on a subscription basis or for a fee

- Applicant's basic fee schedule, how fees are charged, and whether its fees are negotiable

- When compensation is payable, and if compensation is payable before service is provided, how a client may get a refund or may terminate an investment advisory contract before its expiration date

2. Types of clients — Applicant generally provides investment advice to: *(check those that apply)*

❏ A.   Individuals

❏ B.   Banks or thrift institutions

❏ C.   Investment companies

❏ D.   Pension and profit sharing plans

❏ E.   Trusts, estates, or charitable organizations

❏ F.   Corporations or business entities other than those listed above

❏ G.   Other *(describe on Schedule F)*

3. Types of investments. Applicant offers advice on the following: *(check those that apply)*

   A.   Equity securities
❏   (1) Exchange-listed securities
❏   (2) Securities traded over-the-counter

   B.   Warrants
❏   (1) Securities
❏   (2) Commodities
❏   (3) Foreign issuers

   C.   Corporate debt securities (other than commercial paper)
❏   (1) Tangibles

❏ (2) Intangibles

❏ D. Commercial paper

❏ E. Certificates of deposit

F. Municipal securities
❏ (1) Real estate
❏ (2) Oil and gas interests
❏ (3) Other (explain on Schedule F)

❏ G. Investment company securities:

❏ H. United States government securities

❏ I. Options contracts on:

❏ J. Futures contracts on:

K. Interests in partnerships investing in:
❏ (1) Variable life insurance
❏ (2) Variable annuities
❏ (3) Mutual fund shares

❏ L. Other *(explain on Schedule F)*

---

4. **Methods of analysis, sources of information, and investment strategies.**

   A. Applicant's security analysis methods include: *(check those that apply)*

   ❏ (1) Charting

   ❏ (2) Fundamental

   ❏ (3) Technical

   ❏ (4) Cyclical

   ❏ (5) Other *(explain on Schedule F)*

   B. The main sources of information applicant uses include: *(check those that apply)*

❏ (1) Financial newspapers and magazines

❏ (2) Inspections of corporate activities

❏ (3) Research materials prepared by others

❏ (4) Corporate rating services

❏ (5) Timing services

❏ (6) Annual reports, prospectuses, filings with the Securities and Exchange Commission

❏ (7) Company press releases

❏ (8) Other (explain on Schedule F)

C. The investment strategies used to implement any investment advice given to clients include: *(check those that apply)*

❏ (1) Long-term purchases (securities held at least a year)

❏ (2) Short-term purchases (securities sold within a year)

❏ (3) Trading (securities sold within 30 days)

❏ (4) Short sales

❏ (5) Margin transactions

❏ (6) Option writing, including covered options, uncovered options or spreading strategies

❏ (7) Other *(explain on Schedule F)*

---

5. Education and business standards.

Are there any general standards of education or business experience that applicant requires of those involved in determining or giving investment advice to clients? .... ❏ Yes ❏ No

(If yes, please describe these standards on Schedule F)

6. Education and business background.

For:
- Each member of the investment committee or group that determines general investment advice to be given to clients, or
- If the applicant has no investment committee or group, each individual who determines general investment advice
- Clients (if more than five, respond only for their supervisors)
- Each principal executive officer of applicant or each person with similar status or performing similar functions

On Schedule F, give the:
- Name
- Formal education after high school
- Year of birth
- Business background for the preceding five years

7. Other business activities. *(Check those that apply.)*

❏ A.   Applicant is actively engaged in a business other than giving investment advice.

❏ B.   Applicant sells products or services other than investment advice to clients.

❏ C.   The principal business of applicant or its principal executive officers involves something other than providing investment advice.

(For each checked box, describe the other activities, including the time spent on them, on Schedule F.)

8. Other financial industry activities or affiliations. *(Check those that apply.)*

❏ A.   Applicant is registered (or has an application pending) as a securities broker-dealer.

❏ B.   Applicant is registered (or has an application pending) as a futures commission merchant, commodity pool operator, or commodity trading adviser.

❏ C.   Applicant has arrangements that are material to its advisory business or its clients with a related person who is a:

❏ (1)   Broker-dealer .... ❏ Yes   ❏ No

❏ (2)   Investment company .... ❏ Yes   ❏ No

❏ (3)   Other investment advisor .... ❏ Yes   ❏ No

❏ (4)   Financial planning firm .... ❏ Yes   ❏ No

❏ (5)   Commodity pool operator, commodity trading
advisor or futures commission merchant .... ❏ Yes   ❏ No

❏ (6)   Banking or thrift institution .... ❏ Yes   ❏ No

❏ (7)   Accounting firm .... ❏ Yes   ❏ No

❏ (8)   Law firm .... ❏ Yes   ❏ No

❏ (9)   Insurance company or agency .... ❏ Yes   ❏ No

❏ (10) Pension consultant .... ❏ Yes   ❏ No

❏ (11) Real estate broker or dealer .... ❏ Yes   ❏ No

❏ (12) Entity that creates or packages limited
partnerships .... ❏ Yes   ❏ No

*(For each checked box in C, on Schedule F identify the related person
and describe the relationship and the arrangements.)*

❏ D.   Is applicant or a related person a
general partner in any partnership in
which clients are solicited to invest? .... ❏ Yes   ❏ No

(If yes, describe on Schedule F the partnerships and what they invest in.)

9. Participation or interest in client transactions.

Applicant or a related person: *(check those that apply)*

❏ A.   As principal, buys securities for itself from or sells securities it owns to any client

❏ B.   As broker or agent effects securities transactions for compensation for any client

❏ C.   As broker or agent for any person other than a client effects transactions in which client securities are sold to or bought from a brokerage customer

❏ D.   Recommends to clients that they buy or sell securities or investment products in which the applicant or a related person has some financial interest

❏ E.   Buys or sell for itself securities it also recommended to clients

(For each box checked, describe on Schedule F when the applicant or a related person engages in these transactions and what restrictions, internal procedures, or disclosures are used for conflicts of interest in those transactions.)

Describe, on Schedule F, your code of ethics, and state that you will provide a copy of your code of ethics to any client or prospective client upon request.

---

10. **Conditions for managing accounts.** Does the applicant provide investment advisory services, manage investment advisory accounts, or hold itself out as providing financial planning or some similarly termed services and impose a minimum dollar value of assets or other condition for starting or maintaining an account? .... ❏ Yes ❏ No

(If yes, describe on Schedule F)

---

11. **Review of accounts.** If applicant provides investment supervisory services, manages investment advisory account, or holds itself out as providing financial planning or some similarly termed services:

A.   Describe below the reviews and reviewers of the accounts. For reviews, include their frequency, different levels, and triggering factors. For reviewers, include the number of reviewers, their titles and functions, instructions they receive from applicant on performing reviews, and number of accounts assigned each.

B. Describe below the nature and frequency of regular reports to clients on their accounts.

12. Investment or brokerage discretion.

A. Does applicant or any related person have authority to determine, without obtaining specific client consent, the:

(1) Securities to be bought or sold?........................... ❏ Yes ❏ No

(2) Amount of securities to be bought or sold? .... ❏ Yes ❏ No

(3) Broker or dealer to be used? .... ❏ Yes ❏ No

(4) Commission rates paid? .... ❏ Yes ❏ No

B. Does applicant or a related person suggest brokers to clients?... ❏ Yes ❏ No

For each yes answer to A, describe on Schedule F any limitations on the authority.

For each yes to A(3), A(4) or B, describe on Schedule F the factors considered in selecting brokers and determining the reasonableness of their commissions. If the value of products, research, and services given to the applicant or a related person is a factor, describe:

- The products, research, and services

- Whether clients may pay commissions higher than those obtainable from other brokers in return for those products and services

- Whether research is used to service all of applicant's accounts or just those accounts paying for it; and

- Any procedures the applicant used during the last fiscal year to direct client transactions to a particular broker in return for product and research services received.

---

13. Additional compensation.

Does the applicant or a related person have any arrangements, oral or in writing, where it:

A. Is paid cash by or receives some economic benefit (including commissions, equipment or non-research services) from a non-client in connection with giving advice to clients? .... ❏ Yes ❏ No

B. Directly or indirectly compensates any person for client referrals?... ❏ Yes ❏ No

(For each yes, describe the arrangements on Schedule F.)

---

14. Balance sheet. Applicant must provide a balance sheet for the most recent fiscal year on Schedule G if applicant:

- Has custody of client funds or securities (unless applicant is registered or registering only with the Securities and Exchange Commission); or

- Requires prepayment of more than $500 in fees per client and 6 or more months in advance

Has applicant provided a Schedule G balance sheet?.. ❏ Yes ❏ No

(Do not use this Schedule as a continuation sheet for Form ADV Part I or any other Schedules)

1. Full name of applicant exactly as stated in Item 1A of Part I of Form ADV: IRS Employer Identification No.:

Item of form (identify)	Answer

Glossary

Advertising: Paid communication with the specific purpose of promoting a product or service

Baby boomer: Someone who was born during the demographic baby boom following World War II from 1947 to 1964

Benchmark: A standard by which something can be measured. In financial planning, this may be how you measure the services you offer to clients, such as how your service compares to the top financial planning firms.

Brand: The recognized feature or mark that helps distinguish your product or service from others in the eyes of the consumer

Brokers: Temporary wholesalers, paid by fee or commission, who introduce buyers and sellers and facilitate transactions

Business owners policy (BOP): An insurance policy that combines several types of business insurance for which you pay a single premium and receive coverage for a variety of risks associated with owning a business

Business plan: A carefully presented description of your business, your target market, your financials, and your prospects in business.

CFP: Certified Financial Planner, a certification issued by the Financial Planning Board of Standards. To become CFP certified, applicants must pass the comprehensive CFP Certification Examination, pass the CFP Board's *Candidate Fitness Standards*, agree to abide by the CFP Board's *Code of Ethics and Professional Responsibility*, and comply with the *Financial Planning Practice Standards*. Beyond passing the exam, education and experience must be met. CFP candidates must have a bachelor's degree (or higher) from an accredited college or university. Three years of full-time personal financial planning experience also is required.

Competitive advantage: A primary strength or an aspect of your service or product that surpasses the strengths of competitors

Demographics: Population characteristics

Differentiation: Describing what is unique about your service or business

Entrepreneur: A person who creates a new business, venture, or idea and usually assumes the risk for that business venture

Fictitious name: A business name other than the personal name of the business owner

Financial planner: A professional financial adviser who helps clients with various personal financial issues through proper financial planning. This includes, but is not limited to, managing cash flow and planning for the costs associated with estate management, education, retirement, investment, risk management, insurance, and taxes.

Independent contractor: One who offers services using his or her own means

Investment companies: An old term for mutual funds

Innovation: Openness to trying new or possibly risky approaches

IT: Information technology

Investment Advisors Act of 1940: A law that required investment advisers to register with the Securities and Exchange Commission (SEC)

Joint venture: A strategic alliance or agreement of business entities to work together

Limited liability company (LLC): A legal structure for small businesses in which revenue passes through to the business owners, but they are not personally responsible for liabilities incurred by the company.

Marketing: The act of promoting awareness of a product or service to the audience the product or service is meant for

Marketing/marketing communications plan: A written road map or guide that describes how you plan to effectively position and promote your services while distinguishing them from the services of competitors

MP3 file: A patented digital encoding format used for audio files

Mutual fund: An investment fund that sells shares to individual investors and pools the money to invest in stocks, bonds, and other assets

Niche market: A segment of the mainstream market whose business you cultivate

Non-compete clause: A clause in a business sale contract that prohibits the seller of a business from taking existing clients and setting up a new business

OPM: An acronym for "other people's money," which is what a financial planner uses as the basis for his or her work. A financial adviser works with managing the finances of others to help those individuals learn proper financial management.

Outsourcing: Using an outside company or workforce to perform a function that could be done or previously has been done internally

Partnership: A business owned by two or more individuals

Price: An established representation of the value of a product or service

Profit: The positive gain from a business operation, which is calculated by subtracting all business expenses from business income. If the answer to the calculation is positive, then this is a profit. A negative number is a loss.

Promotion: A message used to advertise or market the value of a product or service to its intended consumer or audience

Retail: Involved with sale to the consumer for personal or household use

ROI: Return on investment, comparing net benefits to the total cost of services. Financial planners use ROI to determine how valuable investments are for clients as well as how investing their own money into business expenses such as marketing and other initiatives performs for the business.

Securities and Exchange Commission (SEC): The federal agency responsible for regulating the stock markets

Social media: Online community or group of users where people can connect and communicate with others

Sole proprietorship: A business wholly owned and operated by a single individual

SWOT analysis: A strategic analysis tool for understanding a company's situation by closely examining its internal strengths (S) and weaknesses (W) and its external opportunities (O) and threats (T)

Target market: A customer group whose business a company is seeking to win through a marketing program. The individuals or group of individuals that benefit from the product or service a company or organization is offering.

USP: Unique selling proposition — the unique quality or service that sets your business apart from others.

Useful Websites

Associations and Professional Organizations

American Institute of Certified Public Accountants (AICPA) (**www.aicpa.org**)

Certified Financial Planner Board of Standards, Inc. (**www.cfp.net**)

Chartered Financial Analysts Institute (CFA Institute) (**www.cfainstitute.org**)

Chartered Institute of Management Accountants (CIMA) (**www.cimaglobal.com**)

Financial Industry Regulatory Authority (FINRA) (**www.finra.org**)

Financial Planning Association (or FPA) (**www.fpanet.org**)

Institute of Advanced Financial Planners (**www.iafp.ca**)

Investment Management Consultants Association (IMCA)
(**www.imca.org**)

National Association of Personal Financial Advisors (NAPFA)
(**www.napfa.org**)

National Association of Securities Dealers (NASD) — now FINRA

National Endowment for Financial Education (**www.nefe.org**)

NICCP (National Institute of Certified College Planners)
(**www.niccp.com**)

NIST (National Institute of Standards and Technology) (**www.nist.gov**)

Business Registration

Business Licenses and Permits Search Tool
(**www.sba.gov/content/search-business-licenses-and-permits**)

SCORE (Service Corps of Retired Executives) (**www.score.org**)

U.S. Small Business Administration (**www.sba.gov**)

Domain Name Registration

GoDaddy.com (**www.godaddy.com**)

InterNIC (**http://internic.net/whois.html**)

Network Solutions (**www.networksolutions.com**)

Financing

3iC LLC (**www.help-finance.com/who1.htm**)

Fundingpost.com (**www.fundingpost.com**)

SBA. *How to Prepare a Loan Package.*
(**http://archive.sba.gov/smallbusinessplanner/start/financestartup/
SERV_LOANPACKAGE.html**)

Hiring Employees

BackPage (**www.backpage.com**)

CareerBuilder (**www.careerbuilder.com**)

Craigslist (**www.craigslist.org**)

Elance.com (**www.elance.com**)

Freelancer.com (**www.freelancer.com**)

IFreelance.com (**www.ifreelance.com**)

Kijiji (**www.ebayclassifieds.com**)

Monster (**www.monster.com**)

Sologig.com (**www.sologig.com**)

Yahoo! (**www.yahoo.com**)

Home Office

Craigslist (**www.craigslist.org**)

Insurance

Department of the Treasury's Listing of Approved Sureties (Department Circular 570) (**www.fms.treas.gov/c570/c570.html**)

Employee Dishonesty Bonds.com
(**www.employeedishonestybonds.com**)

FastBusinessInsurance.com
(**www.fastbusinessinsurance.com/types/financial-planner**)

Worldwide Insurance Specialists
(**www.bond007.net/employee-dishonesty-bond.html**)

Information Security

05-49 NASD Reminds Members of Their Obligations Relating to the Protection of Customer Information. FINRA. (**http://finra.complinet.com/en/display/display. html?rbid=2403&record_id=3646&element_id=3198&highlight=int ernet#r3646**)

Consumer Protection Bureau. *Protecting Personal Information: A Guide for Business* (**http://business.ftc.gov/documents/ bus69-protecting-personal-information-guide-business**)

Financial Institutions and Customer Information: Complying with the Safeguards Rule
(**http://business.ftc.gov/documents/bus54-financial-institutions-and-customer-information-complying-safeguards-rule**)

Kissel, Robert. *Small Business Information Security: The Fundamentals.* NIST (**http://csrc.nist.gov/publications/nistir/ir7621/nistir-7621.pdf**)

Security Management & Assurance (**http://csrc.nist.gov/groups/SMA/index.html**)

Marketing

Logo Design

Guru Corporation's Logosnap.com (**www.logosnap.com**)

HP's Logomaker (**www.logomaker.com**)

Business cards

48hourprint.com (**www.48hourprint.com**)

Vistaprint (**www.vistaprint.com**)

Pricing

Costhelper.com (**www.costhelper.com/cost/finance/financial-planner.html**)

Payscale.com (**www.payscale.com/research/US/ Job=Personal_Financial_Advisor/Salary**)

U.S. Bureau of Labor Statistics *Occupational Outlook Handbook* (**www.bls.gov/oco**)

Publications

Bank Investment Consultant (**www.bankinvestmentconsultant.com**)

"Handy Reference Guide to the Fair Labor Act." (**www.dol.gov**)

Investment News: The Leading News Source for Financial Planners(**www.investmentnews.com**)

Journal of Financial Planning: The Official Publication of the Financial Planning Association (**www.fpanet.org/journal**)

Small Business Resource Guide (**www.hud.gov/offices/osdbu/resource/guide.cfm**)

Research

American Community Survey (**www.census.gov/acs**)

American FactFinder (**http://factfinder.census.gov**)

CenStats Databases (**http://censtats.census.gov**)

Chamber of Commerce — Use online search on Business Finance.com (**www.businessfinance.com/chambers-of-commerce.htm**)

County Business Patterns (**www.census.gov/econ/cbp/index.html**)

Demographics Now (**www.demographicsnow.com**)

FINRA — Check brokers background (**www.finra.org/Investors/ToolsCalculators/BrokerCheck/index.htm**)

SEC EDGAR database (**www.sec.gov/edgar.shtml**)

U.S. Bureau of Labor Statistics (**www.bls.gov**)

U.S. Census Bureau (**www.census.gov**)

Standards and Education

Professional Standards of Practice for R.F.Ps. Institute of Advanced Financial Planners (**www.iafp.ca/content.php?SectionID=1&ContentID=33**)

"Understanding Professional Designations." FINRA. (**http://apps.finra.org/DataDirectory/1/prodesignations.aspx**)

Taxes

"Independent Contractor (Self-Employed) or Employee?" on the IRS website (**www.irs.gov/businesses/small/article/0,,id=99921,00.html**)

IRS Publication 587, Business Use of Your Home (**www.irs.gov/pub/irs-pdf/p587.pdf**)

IRS Publication (Circular E), Employer's Tax Guide (**www.irs.gov/pub/irs-pdf/p15.pdf**)

Self-Employed Individuals Tax Center (**www.irs.gov/businesses/small/article/0,,id=115045,00.html#obligations**)

Website design

Adobe Dreamweaver (**www.adobe.com/products/dreamweaver.html**)

Advisor Resources (**http://advisorresources.net**)

Audacity (**http://audacity.sourceforge.net**)

Buildfree.org (**www.buildfree.org**)

Financial Advisor Website Design
(**http://financialadvisorwebsitedesign.com**)

GoDaddy.com (**www.godaddy.com**)

GoToWebinar (**www.gotomeeting.com/fec**)

iLinc (**www.ilinc.com**)

LAME (**http://lame.sourceforge.net/index.php**)

Microsoft Publisher (**http://office.microsoft.com/en-us/publisher**)

RecordForAll (**www.recordforall.com**)

Smarsh (**www.financialvisions.com**)

YouTube (**www.youtube.com**)

Weebly.com (**www.weebly.com**)

Wix.com (**www.wix.com**)

WordPress.com (**http://wordpress.com**)

Search engines

DMOZ Open Directory Project (**http://search.dmoz.org**)

Google (**www.google.com**)

Microsoft's Bing (**www.bing.com**)

Bibliography

05-49 NASD Reminds Members of Their Obligations Relating to the Protection of Customer Information. FINRA. 2005 **http://finra.complinet.com/en/display/display.html?rbid=2403& record_id=3646&element_id=3198&highlight=internet#r3646**.

The A-Z Guide to Federal Employment Laws For the Small Business Owner. Atlantic Publishing Group, Inc., 2010.

Anthony, Mitch. *Your Clients for Life: The Definitive Guide to Becoming a Successful Financial Planner,* 2nd Ed. Dearborn Trade Publishing, 2006.

Brown, Bruce C. *Google Income: How ANYONE of Any Age, Location, and/or Background Can Build a Highly Profitable Online Business with Google.* Atlantic Publishing Group, Inc., 2009.

Brown, Bruce C. *How to Build Your Own Web Site With Little or No Money: The Complete Guide for Business and Personal Use.* Atlantic Publishing Group, Inc. 2009.

Brown, Douglas Robert. *The Restaurant Manager's Handbook: How to Set Up, Operate, and Manage a Financially Successful Food Service Operation* 4th Edition — With Companion CD-ROM. Atlantic Publishing Group, Inc., 2007.

Castle, Janessa. *Your Complete Guide to Making Millions with Your Simple Idea or Invention: Insider Secrets You Need to Know*. Atlantic Publishing Group, Inc., 2010.

Cohen, Sharon L. *199 Internet-Based Businesses You Can Start with Less than One Thousand Dollars: Secrets, Techniques, and Strategies Ordinary People Use Every Day to Make Millions*. Atlantic Publishing Group, Inc., 2010.

Cohen, Sharon L. *Amazon Income: How ANYONE of Any Age, Location, and/or Background Can Build a Highly Profitable Online Business with Amazon*. Atlantic Publishing Group, Inc., 2009.

Cohen, Sharon L. *Yahoo Income: How ANYONE of Any Age, Location, and/ or Background Can Build a Highly Profitable Online Business with Yahoo*. Atlantic Publishing Group, Inc., 2009.

Examinations of Broker-Dealers Offering Online Trading: Summary of Findings and Recommendations. Office of Compliance Inspections and Examinations. 2001. **www.sec.gov/news/studies/online.htm#P140_28099**.

Financial Institutions and Customer Information: Complying with the Safeguards Rule. Federal Trade Commission. 2006. **http://business.ftc.gov/documents/bus54-financial-institutions-and-customer-information-complying-safeguards-rule.**

Fontana, PK. *Choosing the Right Legal Form of Business: The Complete Guide to Becoming a Sole Proprietor, Partnership, LLC, or Corporation.* Atlantic Publishing Group, Inc., 2010.

Gater, Laura. *How to Open & Operate a Financially Successful Medical Billing Service: With Companion CD-ROM.* Atlantic Publishing Group, Inc., 2010.

How to Open & Operate a Financially Successful Landscaping, Nursery, or Lawn Service Business: With Companion CD-ROM. Atlantic Publishing Group, Inc., 2009.

Kissel, Robert. *Small Business Information Security: The Fundamentals. National Institute of Standards and Technology.* 2009. **http://csrc.nist.gov/publications/nistir/ir7621/nistir-7621.pdf.**

Legal Resources. Bureau of Consumer Protection Resources Center. **http://business.ftc.gov/legal-resources/46/33.**

Leone, Diane. *How to Open & Operate a Financially Successful Interior Design Business.* Atlantic Publishing Group, Inc., 2009.

Lovelady, Larisa. *The Complete Guide to Google AdWords: Secrets, Techniques, and Strategies You Can Learn to Make Millions.* Atlantic Publishing Group, Inc., 2010.

Maeda, Martha. *The Complete Guide to Spotting Accounting Fraud & Cover-Ups: Everything You Need to Know Explained Simply.* Atlantic Publishing Group, Inc., 2010.

Manresa, Maritza. *How to Open & Operate a Financially Successful Import Export Business: With Companion CD-ROM.* Atlantic Publishing Group, Inc., 2010.

Nissenbaum, Martin, Barbara J. Raasch, and Charles L. Ratner. *Ernst & Young's Personal Financial Planning Guide.* 5th Ed. John Wiley & Sons, Inc., 2004.

Peter, J. Paul and James H, Donnelly Jr. *Marketing Management Knowledge and Skills.* 6th Ed. Irwin McGraw Hill, 2001.

Protecting Personal Information: A Guide for Business. Federal Trade Commission. **http://business.ftc.gov/documents/bus69-protecting-personal-information-guide-business**.

Rattner, Jeffrey H. *Getting Started as a Financial Planner.* New York: Bloomberg Press, 2005.

Rose, Bryan. *How to Open & Operate a Financially Successful Photography Business: With Companion CD-ROM.* Atlantic Publishing Group, Inc., 2010.

Security Management & Assurance. National Institute of Standards and Technology. 2009. **http://csrc.nist.gov/groups/SMA/index.html**.

Smith-Daughety, Desiree. *Using Other People's Money to Get Rich: Secrets, Techniques, and Strategies Investors Use Every Day Using OPM to Make Millions.* Atlantic Publishing Group, Inc., 2010.

Author Information

Peg Stomierowski

A career writer, editor, and columnist, Peg Stomierowski moved west from New York to Colorado and Alaska. She holds a B.A. degree in journalism from St. Bonaventure University and an MBA degree in leadership/human resource management, marketing, and services management from the University of Colorado. She often has written about businesspeople,  health care, small business, and career development. Peg is a member of American Independent Writers, and she authors an association's blog for Smartbrief.com in Washington, D.C. You can contact Peg at **www.wiredtowrite.biz** or ps@wiredtowrite.biz.

Kristie Lorette

A copywriter and marketing consultant, Kristie Lorette is passionate about helping entrepreneurs and businesses create copy and marketing pieces that sizzle, motivate, and sell. It is through her more than 14 years of experience working in various roles of marketing, financial services, real estate, and event planning that Lorette developed her widespread expertise in advanced business and marketing strategies and communications. Lorette earned a B.S. in marketing and B.S. in multinational business from Florida State University and her M.B.A. from Nova Southeastern University.

Martha Maeda

Martha Maeda has lived and worked in Australia, Japan, Latin America, and several African countries. She currently lives with her family in Orlando, Florida.

Index